THE
BEST
FOODS
OF RUSSIA

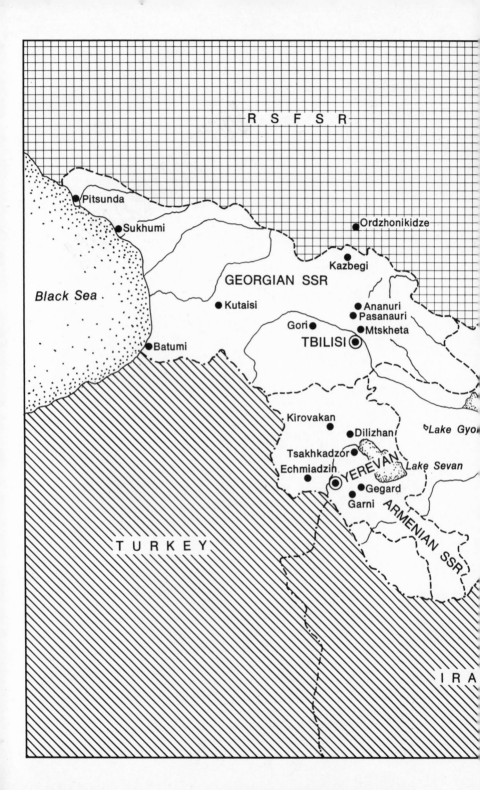

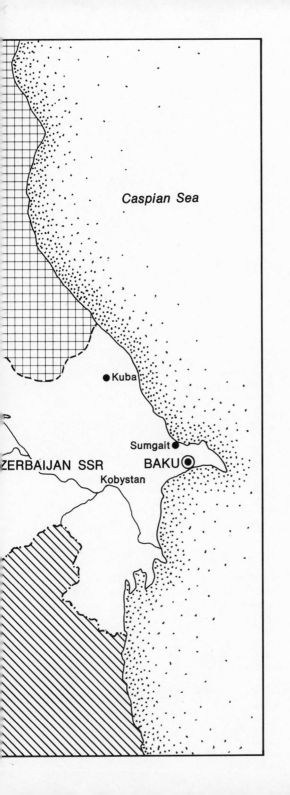

Also by Sonia Uvezian

THE CUISINE OF ARMENIA

THE
BEST
FOODS
OF RUSSIA

Sonia Uvezian

HARCOURT BRACE JOVANOVICH

NEW YORK AND LONDON

Printed in the United States of America

Library of Congress Cataloging in Publication Data
Uvezian, Sonia.
    The best foods of Russia.

    Includes index.
    1. Cookery, Russian. I. Title.
TX723.4.U9   641.5'947   76-12463
ISBN: 0-15-111905-8

First edition
BCDE

ACKNOWLEDGEMENTS

I would like to express my gratitude to Dr. Alexander Leaf of the Harvard
Medical School and Massachusetts General Hospital and to Dr. Ralph
Nelson of the Mayo Clinic, Rochester, Minnesota for their warm and
positive response to the manuscript. To Professor and Mme. Yevgeni
Gerzenstein I extend my sincere appreciation for their kind interest and
assistance. I wish to thank Dr. Stephen Marks and Dr. and Mrs. Herbert
Zimmermann, Jr. for graciously examining the manuscript and lending
their support to this project. Many thanks are also due my publisher and
all those at Harcourt Brace Jovanovich who helped make the production
of this book an enjoyable and rewarding experience for me. I am deeply
indebted to them for their enthusiasm and conscientious thoroughness.

    There are two special people without whose unwavering encour-
agement and invaluable aid this book could not have come into being:
Constance Schrader, who began as my editor and who has become a loyal
and trusted friend, and my husband David, who participated in every
step of its creation and who was, in effect, a virtual collaborator.

                                                        Sonia Uvezian

CONTENTS

THE
BEST
FOODS
OF RUSSIA

To those geniuses of the kitchen,
the incomparable cooks of the Caucasus

INTRODUCTION

The book you are holding is one for which I searched many years, ever since I left my homeland in the Middle East. Not finding it, I ended up writing it. My preoccupation with Caucasian food began with a desire to re-create the unique specialties I had savored or heard about as a child, which had made an impression of depth and fascination that no other style of cooking seemed able to challenge. However, it was not until I was doing research on Caucasian (Eastern) Armenian recipes for my first book, *The Cuisine of Armenia,* in which I concentrated primarily on Western Armenian dishes, that I really came to appreciate the genius and greatness of the region's cuisine.

Today, when there seems to be a cookbook on virtually every conceivable (and inconceivable) subject, it is astonishing that so little has appeared on the ancient and remarkable cuisine of the Caucasus, one of the most fantastically varied, exotic, healthful, and delicious ever devised and one that certainly deserves a place of honor among the great cuisines of the world.

A land of magnificent scenery, of historic and archaeological treasures, fabulous Oriental rugs, and of more than four millennia of recorded history, the Caucasus is the seat of ancient civilizations and the location of the present-day Soviet republics of Armenia, Azerbaidzhan, and Georgia, which occupy a bridge between Russia, Iran, and Turkey.

Few other areas in the world of the same size contain such a diversity of ethnic groups, many with their own language and customs. In Yerevan, the capital of Soviet Armenia, not only five different languages but five different alphabets are used. Although far-reaching changes have taken place in the Caucasus during the past several decades, the peoples of the region continue to cherish and preserve their traditional customs and foods. Caucasian cooking is famous throughout the Soviet Union, and many dishes such as *shashlik*, chicken *tabaka*, and lamb *chakhokhbili* appear regularly on Russian menus. Some of the most popular restaurants in Moscow and other large cities of the USSR specialize in Armenian and Georgian cuisine, and many Russian markets are now featuring pomegranates, figs, and other exotic fruit from the Caucasus.

Caucasian food has its roots deep in antiquity and has both influenced and been influenced by the many peoples—Greeks, Romans, Persians, Arabs, Central Asians, and Turks—who have passed through the land. Fragrant with the aroma of spices and herbs and ranging from earthy peasant fare to noble creations, the glorious cuisine of the Caucasus abounds in succulent kebabs, luscious stuffed vegetables and fruits, dazzling pilafs, and exquisite honeyed sweets that have been perfected by generations of ingenious cooks over a period of many centuries.

The Caucasus is noted for the high average life span of its inhabitants, some of whom live to be 130 years old and more. Every so often one reads about a current "oldest citizen" there. Scientists and newspapermen regularly journey to the Caucasus to study the life-style of the people and their diet, which is filled with natural, health-building foods, including fresh vegetables and herbs, fruits, milk products, nuts, cracked wheat, and honey, which often replaces sugar.

In this richest area of the Soviet Union, an abundance of the finest raw ingredients is to be found. While the principal grain crop of Armenia is wheat, rice cultivated in Azerbaidzhan has long been famous far beyond its borders, and in western Georgia corn is grown for food by nearly every valley peasant. Vegetables and fruits of almost every kind and of the highest quality grow in great profusion throughout the Caucasus. Citrus plantations lie along Georgia's warm and humid Black Sea coast, groves of tangerines, pomegranates, and figs thrive by the shore of the Caspian in Azerbaidzhan, and apricots and peaches from the Ararat plain are the pride of Armenian fruit growers. In the mountain valleys there are vineyards as well as apple, pear, plum, and walnut orchards, and in the warmer regions are found quinces, persimmons, olives, dates, and other fruits. Over 90 percent of the tea produced in the Soviet Union is cultivated in Georgia, and the Apsheron Peninsula in Azerbaidzhan is the only place in the USSR where saffron is grown.

All three republics share a preference for lamb. Beef and veal are eaten to a lesser extent, while pork is traditionally consumed only by the Christian population since the Muslim faith forbids its use. Apart from their talent with meat cookery, Caucasians have created many splendid dishes for poultry and a repertoire of truly aristocratic recipes for game, which is found in great number and variety. Fish dishes are wonderfully diverse as well. The finest caviar in the world comes from the Caspian Sea, and trout from Armenia's Lake Sevan is considered a prized delicacy famous throughout the USSR.

Caucasians seem to have a genius for achieving an exotic end result without recourse to complicated procedures, odd ingredients, and eccentric combinations. It is often the delightfully unexpected addition of a fruit, herb, or a simple spice such as cinnamon rather than something intricate and esoteric that lends charm to so many of their dishes. Caucasian cooking, although it has elements in common with Middle Eastern, has an individual style of its own, with many extraordinary recipes not to be found elsewhere. When a dish is common to both areas, the Caucasian version, though little known, is wonderfully original and subtle.

Herbs and spices commonly used include parsley, coriander, dill, tarragon, mint, basil, oregano, cinnamon, cloves, cumin, saffron, paprika, and various kinds of pepper. For tartness, in addition to vinegar and lemon juice, the Caucasian cook uses sour pomegranate seeds or juice, *abgora* (page 263), and *sumakh* (page 266). Onions, garlic, and tomatoes play an important role in seasoning, and fresh and dried fruits, walnuts, pine nuts, honey, and rose water are essential to many dishes. The amounts given for seasonings may be modified to suit individual taste. However, in order to retain authenticity they should not be omitted. The flavor of a number of Caucasian dishes is enhanced by the use of wine and brandy. Although olive oil is occasionally used, the basic cooking oils of the Caucasus are vegetable and sunflower seed oil. Ordinary butter as well as clarified butter are also widely used. In addition, a number of dishes owe their distinctive flavor to *kyurdyuk*, lamb fat taken from under the tail of a certain species of sheep bred in the Caucasus and Central Asia (see page 265).

In the cuisines of Armenia, Georgia, and Azerbaidzhan there are similarities that have persisted for thousands of years. Lamb, eggplant, yogurt, and bread are fixtures in the diet of all Caucasians. But there are differences as well that can be traced to various influences, among them types of food available, tradition, and dietary laws. For instance, whereas Georgians are particularly addicted to corn, Armenians prefer bulghur (cracked wheat) and Azerbaidzhanis favor rice. Two other ingredients for which Georgians seem to have an insatiable appetite are dried beans and walnuts. Although Armenians and Azerbaidzhanis use them too, they tend to be more partial to chick-peas and almonds. Armenians, in addition, are very fond of pine nuts and pistachios, while Azerbaidzhanis make extensive use of chestnuts. The traditional foods of Armenia and Georgia, both Christian nations, include pork while those of Azerbaidzhan, predominantly a Muslim country, are restricted to lamb and beef. The use of saffron, though important in all three countries, is especially emphasized in Azerbaidzhani cookery, and both Armenians and Azerbaidzhanis have many more pastries and confections than the Georgians.

It is true that a number of dishes are common to the three countries; however each one often has its own way of preparing and serving them. For example, spitted chicken, an immense favorite throughout the Caucasus, is traditionally accompanied by Sour Plum Sauce in Georgia, Pomegranate Syrup in Azerbaidzhan, and slices of fresh or pickled cucumbers, tomatoes, and lemons in Armenia, resulting in three totally different-tasting dishes. Sometimes the difference between one country and the others may be no more than a small nuance in seasoning such as the addition or substitution of an herb, spice, or fruit, yet this small detail is significant enough to effect a noticeable change in flavor.

Finally, each of the republics has its own specialties that are not to be found in the cuisines of the other two. All of these differences ensure Caucasian cuisine against monotony and provide a unique and exciting culinary adventure.

Before sampling the vast panorama of Caucasian cuisine,

let us briefly look at some of the history and characteristics of the individual countries.

Armenia

It is difficult to believe that this landlocked republic, a little larger than the state of Maryland, was once a great kingdom that stretched from the Black to the Caspian Sea, encompassing eastern Turkey down to the Mediterranean, part of northwestern Iran, and the northern tip of Iraq. According to ancient legend the country was founded in the vicinity of Lake Van in what is now Turkey by Haig (or Haik), said to be a descendant of Noah. It is after him that the Armenians call themselves Hai and their country Haiastan. The Armenian nation, historically the oldest in the Caucasus, was preceded by the great Hittite Empire of the second millennium B.C. and the kingdom of Urartu, which flourished around 900 to 700 B.C. and which the Armenians assimilated. It is from Urartu that the name Ararat comes down to us, and indeed the magnificent mountain that bears this name has been the symbol of Armenia for almost three thousand years.

Armenia's strategic location in the line of commercial and military routes made it a coveted prize for a long list of conquerors, who devastated its territory with appalling regularity. Although often controlled by and parceled out among ancient superpowers, including Assyria, Persia, Rome, and Parthia, Armenia managed to retain its national identity into the fourteenth century and even had periods of independence, prosperity, and cultural greatness. Around the year A.D. 301 Armenians became the first nation to be converted to Christianity and have staunchly maintained their own church, often with violent and disastrous consequences, in the face of hostility from their non-Christian neighbors. Nevertheless, Armenia achieved a degree of civilization that was one of the highest in Asia Minor. Its great legacy is still highly visible today in the distinctive architecture of Armenian churches; in the richness of the Armenian language, an independent branch of the Indo-European family, with its alphabet dating back sixteen hundred years and its extensive literature; and in the artistic and creative genius of the Armenian people, whose skill with fabrics, ceramics, and metalwork and whose talent in the arts, science, and commerce have been known and admired for many centuries.

With the plundering of their country and the slaughter of its inhabitants such a common occurrence throughout their history, it is not surprising that many Armenians have left, or often escaped, to other lands. Large groups live in the Middle East, and many have settled in Europe, South America, and even Australia and the Orient. Several hundred thousand live and prosper in North America, where they have been known since as early as 1675.

However, the largest number of Armenians, some two million (including over two hundred thousand who have returned to their native land since 1945 from countries all over the world), live in the Soviet Armenian Republic, which occupies most of the northeastern portion of historical Armenia that was under czarist Russian rule. Its geography is in large part mountainous, with the diversity of the terrain causing considerable difference in types of climate. Only a small percentage of land is arable, but this limited amount is carefully cultivated and supports a bountiful variety of crops that thrive in the fields, orchards, and vineyards under Armenia's obliging sun, which in the Ararat valley and on the Sevan plateau shines over three hundred days a year. As with the other two republics, grape-growing is a major branch of agriculture, and Armenian wines and brandies are widely recognized and acclaimed.

Modern Armenia is a veritable storehouse of fabulous relics of the past. Often called an open-air museum, it contains about five thousand monuments in all, many of which have been or are being painstakingly restored. At the same time the country has undergone an astounding transformation that has turned it into one of the most prosperous and progressive areas in the entire Soviet Union. Its capital, Yerevan, has grown in the last fifty-odd years from a jumble of huts to a beautiful, thriving metropolis and a leading Soviet cultural, scientific, and industrial center. A city of great museums, imaginatively designed buildings, and an abundance of greenery, Yerevan lies at the foot of Mount Ararat, whose snow-capped twin peaks have watched over it since its founding in 782 B.C.

Throughout the entire republic Armenians are striving to continue improving and developing their land and its resources while at the same time preserving their culture and traditions. Within this small territory ancient Armenia is truly living through its second spring.

Azerbaidzhan

A land of striking contrasts and scenic beauty, Azerbaidzhan is the largest and most populous of the Caucasian republics, with an area the size of Maine and about five million inhabitants. Settled since Neolithic times, its riches were chronicled by the Assyrians five thousand years ago. An important transit area for the migration of peoples, Azerbaidzhan became a battleground for a succession of invaders, including Romans, Persians, Arabs,

Mongols, and Turks, the last of whom dominated the country from the eleventh century. Known since antiquity for mysterious "leaping fires," the burning of underground and underwater petroleum, eastern Azerbaidzhan was celebrated by Marco Polo, who noted the fires on his travels to China in the fifteenth century. And indeed it is oil by which Azerbaidzhan is still known to much of the outside world.

This abundance of oil along the shores of the Caspian Sea has led to a high degree of industrialization in the vicinity of Baku, the capital of the republic. But the country is also famous for its highly diversified agricultural output and for its cotton, silk, and carpets and other skilled handiwork.

Present-day Azerbaidzhan consists of the smaller and richer northern part of historical Azerbaijan, the larger southern portion of which now lies in Iran. Around 70 percent of the population are Azerbaidzhanis, a people of Tatar stock who speak a language related to Turkish and who follow the Islamic faith. Other peoples include a sizable Armenian minority. In spite of its turbulent history, the country has a long tradition of science and culture and the people are deeply fond of music and poetry.

Baku, on the Apsheron Peninsula, dates back to at least the ninth century. The old section is a living museum of medieval Arab architecture, while most of the city is spacious and modern, with numerous public gardens and parks and handsome buildings and monuments. This sunny seaside metropolis has grown from a sleepy village of a hundred years ago to a proud urban center of one million people, the largest in the Caucasus.

The landscape of Azerbaidzhan varies widely, from subtropical Caspian beaches to alpine meadows to semidesert. Although only 7 percent of the land is cultivated, the republic accounts for 10 percent of the gross agricultural product of the entire Soviet Union. Azerbaidzhan stands second nationally in the raising of cotton. Tobacco and silkworm breeding are also important, and mulberry trees grow on the mountain slopes. Citrus fruits and vegetables flourish in the warm climate of the southeastern lowland, while the northern region is the USSR's largest producer of hazelnuts and walnuts. Azerbaidzhani rice and fruit have been prized since ancient times, as have been grapes, whose cultivation has recently been dramatically increased.

It has frequently been suggested that the location of the Garden of Eden was in Azerbaidzhan (or, possibly, in Armenia). If so, it is no wonder that in modern times this verdant and picturesque republic with its friendly, hospitable people has become one of the most attractive and inviting areas in all the USSR.

Georgia

One of the most distinctive and colorful regions of the Soviet Union, Georgia is perhaps the best known of the Caucasian republics owing to its being a popular tourist area. And undoubtedly there is a great deal in this exciting land to marvel at and to enjoy. Packed into a territory not much bigger than that of West Virginia are subtropical seacoast, temperate fertile valleys, subalpine pastures and woodlands, and the lofty snow-covered peaks of the Caucasus range, all combining to give Georgia an unusually beautiful natural environment.

Much of the land is mountainous, with the notable exception of the plain of Kolkhida in the west along the Black Sea (the location of the ancient state of Colchis, where Jason and the Argonauts journeyed in quest of the

Golden Fleece). The countryside has been a hunters' paradise since the dawn of civilization, and the available farmland yields a veritable cornucopia of agricultural riches. Tea and grapes are the major crops. Georgia is one of the earliest homes of viticulture, and some five hundred varieties of grapes are grown there, from which outstanding wines are produced. The republic leads the USSR in the bottling of labeled table and dessert wines, including some ten million bottles of champagne annually to help slake the Russian thirst for this beverage. Mulberry trees support a long-established silkworm culture, and tung, eucalyptus, and bamboo trees are also cultivated.

The waters of Georgia are both a source of scenic delight and an important factor in the republic's economy. The mountain rivers and streams provide tremendous hydroelectric power reserves for the country's fast-growing energy needs. Numerous therapeutic mineral springs have made Georgia famous as a health center. Beautiful Lake Ritsa is a favorite mountain vacation area, while the lush Black Sea coast is lined with magnificent beaches and many resort hotels.

Georgia has been inhabited since prehistory. At about the time of the Greeks there were two powerful Georgian states: Colchis and Karthli, known in the ancient world as Iberia, to the east. Although Colchis ultimately fell to the Romans, Karthli was able to retain its independence. In A.D. 337, following the conversion of the Armenians and Byzantines, Georgia accepted Christianity, and shortly afterward the Georgian written language developed. Beautiful churches were built, related in architecture to those of the Armenians. However, soon thereafter, Georgia, despite valiant resistance, fell prey to many invasions and subjugations by Persians, Arabs, Seljuks, Mongols, and Turks, with only a few interruptions of peace and independence. During the twelfth and part of the thirteenth centuries, the nation was unified and its boundaries expanded. This was

Georgia's golden age of wealth and power, with a flowering of trade, science, and culture. The country's population then stood at five million, slightly more than that of today, but eventually it dwindled to less than seven hundred thousand by the time Georgia, decimated and on the verge of destruction, voluntarily joined the Russian Empire in 1801.

Like her sister republic Armenia, modern Georgia is undergoing a profound renascence. Her cities are progressive, her industry thriving, and her land bounteous and blooming. Tbilisi (Tiflis), the capital for fifteen hundred years, is a great center of science and the arts and one of the most important Soviet cities, with a population of some nine hundred thousand. Situated on hilly terrain along the banks of the Kura River, Tbilisi contains many carefully preserved architectural monuments, along with impressive new buildings, broad avenues, and lovely public gardens.

Georgians call themselves Kartveli and their country Sakartvelo. Their language is extremely old, unique, and complex but boasts a rich literature. The people, who make up about 70 percent of the republic's citizens, are among the most individual of all Soviet ethnic groups. Intelligent and highly talented, they have consistently produced a high quota of artists, intellectuals, and professionals and are noted for their exquisite craftsmanship in metalwork, pottery, and jewelry. Like their neighbors, Georgians are gracious and hospitable to visitors, providing them with a warm welcome and proudly sharing their delectable national dishes.

1. APPETIZERS

Appetizers belong among the good things in life that no Georgian or Armenian would want to miss. Although there are a number of Azerbaidzhani dishes that can function as hors d'oeuvres, appetizers as such have never played an important role in the republic's cookery. The traditional Azerbaidzhani first course is remarkably uncomplicated and consists of fresh vegetables and herbs—radishes, scallions, tomatoes, cucumbers, watercress, coriander, tarragon, basil, and others. On occasion salads and pickled vegetables are also served as hors d'oeuvres.

In Georgia and Armenia appetizers can be as simple or as elaborate as one chooses, ranging from a small assortment to a vast array that could provide an exciting buffet dinner.

A typical Georgian first course might include some or all of the following: fresh herbs, radishes, scallions, tiny seedless cucumbers and quartered tomatoes (perhaps sprinkled with dill), home-cured olives, pickled cabbage, red kidney beans or some other vegetable dressed with walnut sauce, eggplant puree, pieces of brined cheese or slices of deep-fried cheese with a topping of mint, sturgeon smoked over hickory or boiled and garnished with tarragon, mountain trout fried to a crisp, and smaller versions of the Georgian cheese bread known as *khachapuri*.

The Armenians, in addition to fresh greens, olives, eggplant puree, and brined cheese, have their own specialties: toasted pumpkin seeds; roasted and salted pistachios, almonds, and chick-peas; dried bean puree; salads and pickled vegetables of many kinds; stuffed grapevine leaves, cabbage leaves, and vegetables; pickled fish; fried fish cakes; raw and cooked lamb and wheat balls; egg-stuffed meat rolls; *basturma* (spicy dried beef) and *soudjuk* (Armenian sausage); hot, flaky cheese or meat pastries called *boereg;* and many others.

Both Georgian and Armenian appetizers are accompanied by *lavash*, a thin white bread, and *raki*, a very dry, potent spirit distilled from grapes. Whether served this way or washed down with other alcoholic beverages, you will find that many of these appetizers provide splendid fare for cocktail parties and buffets.

For other appetizers please consult the chapters on salads, egg dishes, savory pastries and pastas, vegetables, pickles, and dairy products.

A Platter of Fresh Herbs

Georgians and Azerbaidzhanis are immensely fond of fresh herbs and serve a wide assortment as a first course.

One corner of every Caucasian garden is certain to be devoted to the cultivation of a large variety of herbs and greens, of which some have no English name since they are found only in the Caucasus.

Wash sprigs of fresh parsley, basil, mint, dill, coriander, tarragon, or any other herbs you like, and arrange them on a platter. Serve without dressing, alone or with other appetizers. Fresh herbs are also delicious eaten with bread, cheese, scallions, cucumbers, tomatoes, and radishes. A favorite sandwich with Caucasians is brined cheese and fresh herbs rolled in the thin bread called *lavash* (page 221).

Eggplant Puree

In its many variations this popular dish, sometimes called "poor man's caviar," is one of the most famous Caucasian appetizers.

Serves 4

1 large eggplant (about 2 pounds)
3 tablespoons freshly squeezed and strained lemon juice
2 tablespoons olive oil
1 small clove garlic, crushed (optional)
2 scallions, finely chopped, including 2 inches of the green tops

Salt and freshly ground black pepper to taste
1 medium tomato, cut into wedges
1 small green pepper, seeded, deribbed, and sliced
8 black olives
1 tablespoon finely chopped parsley and/or fresh dill

Cut the stem and hull from the top of the eggplant and discard. Using a long-handled fork, prick the skin of the eggplant in several places, then insert the fork through it and broil over charcoal or a gas flame, turning it frequently until the flesh is very soft and the skin charred. The eggplant may also be broiled in an electric oven. Place it on a baking sheet and broil 4 inches from the heat about 25 minutes, turning it to char evenly on all sides. It is important that the eggplant be thoroughly cooked inside before mashing it; otherwise it will have a bitter taste, rendering the dish inedible.

When the eggplant is cool enough to handle, gently squeeze it to remove the bitter juices. Peel off the skin, remove the badly charred spots, and slit the eggplant open. Scoop out the seeds and discard. Place the eggplant pulp in a bowl, immediately pour the lemon juice over it, and mash it thoroughly into a smooth puree. Gradually beat in the olive oil, garlic, scallions, and salt and pepper. Taste for seasoning. Spread on a serving dish, cover, and chill. Before serving decorate with the tomato, green pepper, and olives. Sprinkle the parsley and/or dill on top.

● *Variations*
Instead of the tomato, green pepper, black olives, and parsley and/or dill, you may garnish the eggplant puree with fresh pomegranate seeds and minced fresh coriander leaves. Or beat in 1 tablespoon minced coriander leaves with the scallions. Form the eggplant puree into the shape of a fish with glittering pomegranate seed eyes.

EGGPLANT SALAD
Instead of mashing the broiled eggplant into a puree, chop it finely. Add minced scallions, parsley, and dill. Season

with olive oil, lemon juice, and salt and pepper. Mix well, cover, and chill. Serve garnished with the tomato wedges (or cherry tomatoes) and black olives.

Eggplant with Walnuts Armenia [Ungouyzov Patrichan]

Serves 4

1 large eggplant (about 2 pounds)
Salt to taste
½ cup shelled walnuts
1 small clove garlic
Cayenne to taste (optional)
1 tablespoon white wine vinegar

3 tablespoons cold water
1 tablespoon finely chopped parsley
1 medium tomato, cut into wedges

Broil the eggplant as described in the recipe for Eggplant Puree (page 17). Chop the eggplant pulp and season with the salt. Set aside. Pound the walnuts to a paste with the garlic clove and cayenne. Stir in the wine vinegar and water until well blended. Add the eggplant pulp and mix well. Taste for seasoning. Cover and chill. Sprinkle with the parsley, garnish with the tomato wedges, and serve.

• *Variation*
Instead of the tomato wedges, you may garnish the dish with the seeds from a fresh pomegranate.

Spinach and Yogurt Appetizer

Serves 4

1 pound spinach, washed, drained, stemmed, and coarsely chopped

½ cup water

3 tablespoons olive oil

1 small onion, finely chopped

1 cup unflavored yogurt

1 small clove garlic, crushed, or to taste

½ teaspoon crushed dried mint

Salt and freshly ground black pepper to taste

2 tablespoons finely chopped toasted walnut meats

In a heavy saucepan combine the spinach with the water and bring to a boil over high heat. Reduce the heat to low, cover, and simmer 10 minutes. Drain and squeeze the spinach dry. In a heavy skillet heat the oil over moderate flame. Add the onion and sauté until golden, stirring frequently. Add the spinach and sauté a few minutes. Remove from the heat.

In a mixing bowl combine the yogurt, garlic, mint, and salt and pepper until well blended. Gradually stir in the contents of the skillet and mix thoroughly. Taste for seasoning. Transfer to a serving bowl, cover, and chill. Serve sprinkled with the walnuts.

Pickled Beets in Walnut Sauce Georgia

Serves 4 with other appetizers

2 cups Pickled Beets (page
   206)
¾ cup shelled walnuts
2 to 3 cloves garlic,
   crushed
1 teaspoon ground
   coriander

Salt and cayenne to taste
2 to 3 tablespoons liquid
   from the Pickled Beets
Bibb lettuce leaves

Dice the Pickled Beets and reserve. Pound the walnuts to a smooth paste with the garlic cloves, coriander, and salt and cayenne. Stir in enough of the beet liquid, 1 teaspoon at a time, until the mixture attains the consistency of a thick sauce. Taste for seasoning. Add the reserved beets and mix gently but thoroughly, being careful not to bruise them. Serve cold on the lettuce leaves.

Red Beans in Walnut Sauce
[Lobio]

A thoroughly Georgian combination which is usually offered as one of several appetizers.

Serves 4

1 cup dried red kidney
   beans, or 2 cups canned
   red kidney beans

Salt to taste
½ cup shelled walnuts
1 small clove garlic

Cayenne to taste
1 tablespoon wine vinegar
3 tablespoons cold water
2 tablespoons finely
    chopped onion
2 tablespoons finely

chopped fresh coriander
leaves, or ½ teaspoon
ground coriander
2 tablespoons finely
    chopped parsley

If using the dried kidney beans, soak them in water several hours. Drain and rinse. Cover with fresh water and simmer, uncovered, until the beans are tender but still intact. Add boiling water if needed to keep the beans covered during cooking. When done, drain, place in a bowl, and salt to taste. (Canned beans need only to be drained, rinsed under running cold water, and drained again). Set aside.

Pound the walnuts to a paste with the garlic clove and cayenne. Stir in the wine vinegar and water until well blended. Add to the beans along with the onion, coriander, and parsley. Mix well, being careful not to bruise the beans. Cover and chill before serving.

• *Variations*
Instead of the above herbs, a mixture of ½ tablespoon each minced coriander, parsley, mint, and basil may be used. The dish may be accompanied by a platter of trimmed scallions and/or a bowl of fresh coriander, parsley, mint, and basil on the side.

RED BEANS WITH POMEGRANATE JUICE AND WALNUTS
Follow the recipe for Red Beans in Walnut Sauce (above), substituting 5 tablespoons pomegranate juice for the wine vinegar and water. Sprinkle with ½ cup pomegranate seeds just before serving.

Grapevine Leaves Stuffed with Lentils and Bulghur
[Derevapatat or Derevi Dolma (Sarma)]

The numerous Middle Eastern versions of this well-known appetizer are difficult to surpass, but the Caucasian Armenian interpretation that follows is, if possible, even more memorable.

Makes 50 (serves 10 to 12)

⅔ cup sunflower seed oil
  or vegetable oil
1 large onion, finely
  chopped
1 cup cooked lentils
¾ cup coarse bulghur,
  soaked in hot water 30
  minutes and drained
4 sour plums, pitted and
  finely chopped
½ cup seedless raisins or
  dried currants
⅓ cup finely chopped
  fresh herbs (coriander,
  mint, and savory)
Salt and freshly ground
  black pepper to taste
60 fresh, tender grapevine
  leaves or 60 preserved
  leaves (a 1-pound jar)
½ cup dried apricots,
  chopped
1 cup water
Finely chopped parsley

In a heavy skillet heat ⅓ cup of the oil over moderate heat. Add the onion and sauté until golden brown, stirring frequently. Remove from the heat. Add the lentils, bulghur, plums, raisins, herbs, and salt and pepper. Mix well, taste for seasoning, and set aside.

If using fresh grapevine leaves, soak them in boiling salted water 2 minutes to soften, then rinse under cold water. Rinse preserved grapevine leaves in hot water to remove the brine. Spread the washed leaves on absorbent paper to drain.

Cover the bottom of a heavy casserole with 10 of the leaves to prevent the stuffed leaves from burning during cooking. Stuff each of the remaining 50 leaves as follows: Remove the stem, if any, and spread the leaf on a plate, stem end toward you, dull side up. Place about 1 teaspoon (or more for larger leaves) of the bulghur mixture near the stem end. Fold the stem end over the stuffing, then fold over the sides to enclose the stuffing securely. Beginning at the stem end, roll the grapevine leaf firmly away from you toward the tip, forming a cylinder.

Layer the stuffed leaves seam sides down and close together in neat rows in the casserole. Scatter the apricots around them. Mix the remaining ⅓ cup oil with the water and pour over the stuffed leaves. Gently place an inverted plate over the top to keep the stuffed leaves in place while cooking. Bring to a boil over moderate heat. Reduce the heat to low, cover, and simmer about 50 to 60 minutes or until the stuffing is very tender. If necessary, more water may be added. Remove from the heat and cool to room temperature. Remove the plate and arrange the stuffed leaves on a serving platter. Cover and chill. Serve cold, sprinkled with the parsley.

Note: In the Caucasus the native *albukhara* plums are used for this dish. You may pour boiling water over the plums before removing the pits and mincing the pulp.

Raw Lamb and Wheat Balls
[Houm Kiufta]

Those who are fond of garlic will welcome this interesting version of a traditional Armenian dish flavored with garlic rather than onion, as is normally the case.

Serves 4

¾ to 1 cup fine bulghur
½ pound very lean
  boneless leg of lamb,
  ground 3 times
1 to 2 small cloves garlic,
  pureed
Salt, freshly ground black
  pepper, and cayenne to
  taste

½ cup finely chopped
  parsley
¼ cup finely chopped
  scallions, including 2
  inches of the green tops
2 medium tomatoes, cut
  into eighths
1 lemon, cut into wedges

Rinse the bulghur thoroughly in a strainer under running cold water. Squeeze out the moisture and place in a mixing bowl. Add the lamb, garlic, and salt, pepper, and cayenne. Moisten your hands now and then by dipping them into a bowl of ice water and knead the mixture vigorously about 10 minutes or until well blended, moist, and smooth. Or you may pound the mixture in a stone mortar, adding 1 or 2 tablespoons cold water. Taste for seasoning. Keeping hands moist, form the mixture into 1-inch balls and arrange on a serving platter. Sprinkle with the parsley and scallions. Garnish with the tomatoes and lemon wedges. Serve at once.

2. SALADS

Salads are basic to the diet of Caucasians, who serve them at most meals either as a first course or as a side dish. During hot weather the more substantial salads provide refreshing meals suitable for a light lunch or supper.

Raw and cooked vegetables, legumes, eggs, fruits, and wild greens such as purslane are all used in salads. The choice of dressing varies according to the particular salad. Some salads are simply sprinkled with salt, pepper, and fresh herbs and served without dressing. Others are dressed with either oil or vinegar or a combination of oil and vinegar or lemon juice mixed to taste. Occasionally unflavored yogurt is added to the dressing, or yogurt or sour cream may replace the dressing itself. An unusual dressing is walnut sauce, which can transform the most ordinary salad into an exotic delicacy. Common flavorings for salads include garlic, onion, and fresh or dried herbs.

Choose salad greens and vegetables that are fresh and

unbruised. Wash them well under running cold water, dry, and refrigerate until chilled. Always handle greens gently so they will not bruise, and toss them with the dressing at the last possible moment unless directed otherwise in the recipe. Vegetables and legumes used in cooked salads must not be overcooked. When done they should be tender but still somewhat firm, not mushy. These will absorb their dressing better if dressed while still hot.

Since vinegars vary greatly in their quality and strength, it is important to use a good red or white wine vinegar that is not overly strong. The choice of salad oil is also important. Caucasians use sunflower seed, vegetable, and olive oil in dressings. Good brands of each are easily available in this country and may be used in these salads.

Armenian Salad
[Haigagan Aghtsan]

Serves 6

2 medium cucumbers, peeled and sliced

2 medium tomatoes, sliced

1 medium green pepper, seeded, deribbed, and sliced

½ cup thinly sliced mild onion

¼ cup finely chopped parsley

⅓ cup finely chopped fresh basil

2 tablespoons finely chopped fresh coriander leaves (optional)

¼ cup olive oil or sunflower seed oil

2 tablespoons freshly squeezed and strained lemon juice

1 tablespoon red wine vinegar

Salt and freshly ground black pepper to taste

Combine the cucumbers, tomatoes, green pepper, and onion in a salad bowl. Sprinkle with the parsley, basil, and coriander. Beat together the oil, lemon juice, vinegar, and salt and pepper with a fork or whisk until well blended. Pour over the salad and toss gently but thoroughly. Serve at once.

● *Variation*
YEREVAN SALAD (Yerevan Aghtsan)
Omit the green pepper, onion, and coriander. Arrange the cucumber and tomato slices in alternating rows on a serving platter. Garnish with the parsley and basil. This is eaten with or without the dressing spooned over it.

Tossed Salad

Serves 4

4 cups torn romaine lettuce leaves
2 cups torn endive leaves
¼ cup watercress sprigs
1 small cucumber, peeled and thinly sliced (cut out seeds if too large and discard)
16 cherry tomatoes
½ cup seeded, deribbed, and thinly sliced green pepper
12 pitted black olives
¼ cup finely chopped red onion

½ cup coarsely chopped parsley
3 tablespoons olive oil
2 tablespoons freshly squeezed and strained lemon juice
¼ teaspoon dill weed
¼ teaspoon dried basil
¼ teaspoon crushed dried mint
Salt and freshly ground black pepper to taste

Combine the lettuce, endive, watercress, cucumber, tomatoes, green pepper, olives, onion, and parsley in a salad bowl. Cover and refrigerate. Beat together the olive oil, lemon juice, dill weed, basil, mint, and salt and pepper with a fork or whisk until well blended. Let stand ½ hour. Just before serving, beat the dressing ingredients again and pour over the salad. Toss gently but thoroughly and serve.

Note: When available, finely chopped fresh dill, basil, and mint leaves may be substituted for the dried herbs. Add according to taste along with the parsley before tossing with the dressing. Also, the salad may be sprinkled with crumbled feta cheese.

Vegetable Salad with Walnut Sauce
Georgia

A distinctive and original salad to serve with fish, chicken, or turkey.

Serves 3 or 4

1 medium cucumber, peeled, quartered lengthwise (cut out seeds if too large and discard), and thinly sliced
1 medium tomato, seeded and diced
½ cup very thinly sliced celery

Cayenne to taste
1 tablespoon wine vinegar
3 tablespoons cold water
2 tablespoons finely chopped onion
2 tablespoons finely chopped fresh coriander leaves or ½ teaspoon ground coriander
2 tablespoons finely

Salt to taste
½ cup shelled walnuts
1 small clove garlic

chopped parsley
Romaine or Bibb lettuce
leaves

Combine the cucumber, tomato, and celery in a mixing bowl and season with salt. Pound the walnuts to a paste with the garlic clove and cayenne. Stir in the vinegar and water until well blended. Add to the vegetables along with the onion, coriander, and parsley. Mix gently but thoroughly. Taste for seasoning. Serve cold over the lettuce leaves.

Apple, Tomato, and Cucumber Salad

It is the unexpected inclusion of apple that gives this salad its unique taste.

Serves 4

1 medium unpeeled
   apple, cored and diced
2 small tomatoes, seeded
   and cut into small
   pieces
1 medium cucumber,
   peeled, quartered
   lengthwise (cut out
   seeds if too large and
   discard), and diced

1 small sweet onion, cut
   lengthwise in half and
   thinly sliced
2 scallions, thinly sliced,
   including 2 inches of
   the green tops
2 to 3 tablespoons olive oil
Salt to taste
Romaine lettuce leaves

Combine all the ingredients except the lettuce in a salad bowl. Toss gently but thoroughly and serve on the lettuce leaves.

Spinach and Egg Salad with Yogurt

Serves 4

4 cups spinach leaves
2 to 6 scallions, finely
  chopped, including 2
  inches of the green tops
1 cup unflavored yogurt
½ cup olive oil

Salt and freshly ground
  black pepper to taste
4 hard-cooked eggs,
  chopped
12 black olives

Wash the spinach thoroughly. Drain. Dry with paper towels. Shred and combine with the scallions in a salad bowl. Beat the yogurt, olive oil, and salt and pepper with a fork until well blended. Add the eggs. Pour the mixture over the spinach. Mix gently but thoroughly, taking care not to mash the eggs. Taste for seasoning. Garnish with the olives. Serve chilled.

• *Variation*
PLAIN SPINACH SALAD
Combine 1 pound spinach, stemmed and shredded, and ¼ cup minced mild onion in a salad bowl. Add 2 tablespoons freshly squeezed and strained lemon juice, 2 tablespoons olive oil, and salt to taste. Toss well and serve.

Grilled Eggplant, Green Pepper, and Tomato Salad
[Leninakan Aghtsan]

Today as one approaches Leninakan, Armenia's second-largest city, it is difficult to realize that this modern urban center has been continuously inhabited since the Bronze Age. The following recipe comes from Leninakan. To achieve the maximum in flavor, grill the vegetables over a wood or charcoal fire as is done in the Caucasus.

Serves 4

1 eggplant (about 1 pound), cubed

2 medium green peppers, quartered lengthwise, seeded, and deribbed

2 medium tomatoes, quartered lengthwise

2 tablespoons finely chopped onion

2 tablespoons finely chopped parsley

3 tablespoons olive oil

Salt and freshly ground black pepper to taste

1½ tablespoons wine vinegar

Grill the eggplant, green peppers, and tomatoes until they are cooked through, turning frequently. Peel off the skins of the peppers while they are still hot. Combine in a salad bowl with the grilled eggplant and tomatoes. Sprinkle with the onion and parsley. Add the oil and toss gently but thoroughly. Sprinkle with the salt and pepper and the vinegar and mix again. Serve cold as a first course or as an accompaniment to broiled fish or meats.

Asparagus and Egg Salad with Yogurt
Armenia
[Asbourag Aghtsan]

A cool, inviting combination flavored with garlic.

Serves 4

1 pound fresh asparagus
1 hard-cooked egg,
  chopped

Garlic Yogurt Sauce (page
  214)

Snap off the tough ends of the asparagus. Cut into 1-inch pieces. Cover with boiling salted water and boil, uncovered, 15 to 20 minutes or until tender. Drain and cool. Combine with the egg and Garlic Yogurt Sauce and toss lightly. Serve cold.

Potato and Egg Salad with Sour Cream

A rich and appetizing creation that may be served for lunch.

Serves 4

2 medium boiling potatoes
1 medium cucumber,
  peeled, quartered
  lengthwise (cut out
  seeds if too large and
  discard), and diced

1 medium tomato, seeded
  and diced.
2 hard-cooked eggs, cut
  into wedges
3 scallions, finely
  chopped, including 2

inches of the green tops
2 tablespoons finely
  chopped parsley
2 tablespoons finely
  chopped fresh dill

Salt and white pepper to
  taste
1 cup sour cream
Romaine lettuce leaves

Cook the potatoes in boiling salted water until just tender. Drain. Peel when cool enough to handle. Cut into small pieces and place in a mixing bowl. Add the cucumber, tomato, eggs, and scallions. Sprinkle with the parsley, dill, and salt and pepper. Add the sour cream and toss gently but thoroughly. Taste for seasoning. Cover and chill. Serve on the lettuce leaves.

• *Variation*
COLD BOILED LAMB WITH SOUR CREAM (Soyoutma)
This is an Azerbaidzhani dish which consists of slices of cold boiled lamb, onion, and tomato, seasoned with salt and pepper, and bound together with sour cream. For a more interesting and substantial meal, follow the above recipe, adding ¼ pound cold boiled lamb, cut in strips. Use 1 potato, ¼ cucumber, and omit the eggs if you like.

Crab and Potato Salad

Another delectable salad that can also fill the function of a main course.

Serves 4

4 medium boiling potatoes	¼ cup finely chopped parsley
6 tablespoons freshly squeezed and strained lemon juice	½ cup homemade mayonnaise
6 tablespoons olive oil	2 hard-cooked eggs, cut into wedges
Salt and freshly ground black pepper to taste	8 black olives
1 pound fresh crab meat	Parsley sprigs

Cook the potatoes in boiling salted water until just tender. Drain. When cool enough to handle, peel and dice. Sprinkle with the lemon juice, olive oil, and salt and pepper and allow to cool to room temperature. Reserve ½ cup of the crab meat. Add the remaining crab meat and the parsley to the salad and toss gently but thoroughly. Finely chop the reserved crab meat and combine it with the mayonnaise. Spoon over the salad and garnish with the eggs, olives, and parsley sprigs.

● *Variation*
Use 4 eggs rather than 2. Mash the yolks with the mayonnaise. Add the reserved crab meat and mix well. Taste for seasoning. Spoon over the salad and garnish with the olives, parsley sprigs, and the egg whites, which have been finely chopped.

White Bean Salad

Serves 4

1 cup dried white beans
  (Great Northern), or
  substitute 2 cups canned
  white kidney beans
¼ cup olive oil
¼ cup freshly squeezed
  and strained lemon juice
Salt and white pepper to
  taste
2 scallions, finely
  chopped, including 2
  inches of the green tops

1 tablespoon finely
  chopped parsley
1 tablespoon finely
  chopped fresh dill
1 tablespoon finely
  chopped fresh mint
  leaves
1 medium tomato, cut into
  eighths
2 hard-cooked eggs,
  quartered
8 black olives

If you are using the dried beans, soak them overnight in water to cover. Drain and rinse. Cover with fresh water and bring to a boil over high heat. Reduce the heat to low and simmer, uncovered, until the beans are tender but still somewhat firm, not mushy. Add boiling water if needed to keep the beans covered during cooking. (Canned beans need only to be drained, rinsed under running cold water, and drained again.)

In a salad bowl beat together the olive oil, lemon juice, and salt and pepper with a fork or whisk until well blended. Add the drained beans and mix gently but thoroughly. Cover and chill. Before serving sprinkle the scallions, parsley, dill, and mint over the beans. Garnish with the tomato, eggs, and black olives. Serve as an appetizer or as a side dish.

- *Variation*

MASHED WHITE BEAN SALAD

Mash the drained beans or blend to a smooth paste in an electric blender. Beat in the olive oil, lemon juice, and salt and pepper. Cover and chill. Sprinkle with the scallions and 1 tablespoon minced parsley or dill. Garnish with the tomato, eggs, and olives and serve.

3. SOUPS

Among the gastronomic delights of the Caucasus, the phenomenal variety of imaginative soups, ranging from simple country recipes to elegant creations of noble character, is particularly remarkable.

Caucasian soups may be divided into roughly three categories: (1) plain broths made from meat, chicken, fish, or vegetables; (2) sophisticated vegetable purees and cream soups; and (3) thick, stewlike soups incorporating a variety of ingredients, including meat, vegetables, legumes, eggs, fruits, nuts, herbs, and wheat, rice, or some form of pasta.

Soups form an important part of the Caucasian menu. Light soups are served as first courses, while substantial ones are frequently eaten as a meal in themselves.

Typical flavorings for soups include onion, tomato, lemon juice, vinegar, cinnamon, saffron, and yogurt, which imparts a unique, tart taste to a number of ancient and classic Caucasian soups, among them several outstanding ones designed for the hot summer months. Sugar-sweetened cold fruit soups are also summer favorites and can function either as a first course or as a dessert.

Simple garnishes such as fresh coriander, dill, basil, parsley, tarragon, mint, and scallions, minced and sprinkled on top just before serving, lend soups an attractive appearance and a refreshing taste. Other common additions made toward the end of cooking include sautéed minced onion, chopped or ground walnuts, eggs alone or in combination with lemon juice or vinegar for a tangy flavor, and melted or minced *kyurdyuk*, which is unavailable in America and which gives *piti*, an Azerbaidzhani favorite, its distinctive taste. *Piti* is a thick lamb soup traditionally prepared and served in small, individual, earthenware casseroles. Besides lamb and *kyurdyuk* it contains chick-peas, potatoes, onion, sour plums, and saffron or tomatoes. It is served sprinkled with dried mint and accompanied by sliced onions and *sumakh* on the side.

Although the soups in this chapter represent only a fraction of the exceptionally large number that exist in the Caucasus, they have been chosen to show the excellent variety available. The Armenian cuisine alone encompasses well over one hundred soups, and a comprehensive list of Caucasian soups would require a volume all its own.

Some of the soups that follow are remarkably uncomplicated, others are a bit more demanding, but almost all may be prepared in advance and will taste even better the following day. Whether served as a light preamble to a company dinner, as a nourishing and hearty main course for a family meal, or as the chief attraction of a late gathering, Caucasian soups offer a glorious assortment of tastes and textures for those who seek to combine novelty with superb eating.

Pasta Soup with Potato and Saffron
Azerbaidzhan

The saffron and sautéed onion lend a distinctive character to this uncomplicated and appealing soup.

Serves 4

¼ cup butter
1 large onion, finely
   chopped
4 cups chicken broth
Salt to taste
1 medium potato, peeled
   and cut into small cubes

½ cup soup pasta or ¼-
   inch-wide egg noodles
¼ teaspoon powdered
   saffron or to taste

In a small skillet heat the butter over moderate heat. Add the onion and sauté until golden brown, stirring frequently. Remove from the heat and set aside.

In a heavy pot bring the chicken broth to a boil over high heat. Add the salt and potato. Reduce the heat, cover, and cook 10 minutes. Add half the sautéed onion and the pasta and cook 10 minutes or until the potato and pasta are tender. Dissolve the saffron in 1 tablespoon warm water and add to the soup. Stir in the remaining sautéed onion, taste for seasoning, and serve.

Note: This soup is also good without the saffron.

Chilled Yogurt Soup
[Ovdukh]

A healthful and fresh-tasting Azerbaidzhani soup, perfect for a hot summer day.

Serves 4

1 medium cucumber
2 cups unflavored yogurt
1 cup ice water
½ pound cold boiled lean beef, cubed
2 hard-cooked eggs, chopped
4 finely chopped scallions, including 2 inches of the green tops
2 tablespoons finely chopped fresh coriander leaves or parsley
¼ cup finely chopped fresh dill
Salt to taste

Peel the cucumber and halve lengthwise. Cut out the seeds if too large and discard. Slice the cucumber crosswise into ¼-inch pieces and set aside. Pour the yogurt into a deep bowl and stir until smooth. Add the ice water and mix until well blended. Add the reserved cucumber pieces and the remaining ingredients. Mix gently but thoroughly. Taste for seasoning and serve chilled.

Note: *Ovdukh* may also be made without meat.

Yogurt Soup with Meatballs
[Dovga]

Unlike *ovdukh* (p. 41), this richly flavored and popular Azerbaidzhani soup is served hot. It can provide a warming and fortifying meal on a cold winter evening.

Serves 4

½ pound lean beef or lamb, ground twice
1 small onion, grated
Salt and freshly ground black pepper to taste
3 cups unflavored yogurt
1 tablespoon flour
3½ cups beef or lamb broth
¼ cup uncooked long-grain white rice
½ cup drained canned chick-peas, rinsed

1½ cups chopped spinach leaves, or a combination of sorrel and spinach
3 to 4 tablespoons finely chopped fresh coriander leaves or parsley
3 to 4 tablespoons finely chopped fresh dill
3 to 4 tablespoons finely chopped chives or scallions, including 2 inches of the green tops

In a mixing bowl combine the meat, onion, and salt and pepper. Knead with your hands until well blended. Taste for seasoning. Form the mixture into balls about 1 inch in diameter and set aside.

Pour the yogurt into a large, heavy pot. Using a whisk or fork, beat in the flour and then the broth until well blended. Season with the salt and pepper. Bring slowly to a boil, stirring constantly in one direction. When the mixture is thickened slightly, add the meatballs and rice and simmer 10 minutes, stirring frequently. Add the chick-peas and spinach and simmer about 10 minutes or until the meatballs and rice are tender. Stir in the remaining ingredients, taste for seasoning, and cook 5 minutes. Serve hot.

Note: *Dovga* may also be prepared without meat.

Meatball Soup with Rice, Vegetables, and Herbs Armenia
[Kiufta Pozpash]

Serves 4

1 pound lean lamb or beef, ground twice
1 medium onion, grated
1 small egg
6 tablespoons minced fresh dill or a mixture of dill, basil, and coriander or parsley
Salt and freshly ground black pepper to taste
5 tablespoons butter
2 medium onions, finely chopped
4 medium tomatoes, peeled, seeded, and chopped
5 cups beef broth or water
⅔ cup uncooked long-grain white rice
3 medium potatoes, peeled and cubed
1 large green pepper, seeded, deribbed, and diced

In a mixing bowl combine the meat, grated onion, egg, 2 tablespoons of the dill, and salt and pepper. Knead with your hands until well blended. Taste for seasoning. Shape the mixture into 1-inch balls and set aside.

In a large, heavy pot heat the butter over moderate heat. Add the onions and sauté until golden brown, stirring frequently. Add the tomatoes, broth, and salt to taste and bring to a boil over high heat. Add the meatballs, reduce the heat, cover, and cook 10 minutes. Add the rice and potatoes and cook 10 minutes. Add the green pepper and simmer 20 minutes or until the meat and vegetables are tender. If necessary a little more broth may be added. Stir the remaining 4 tablespoons dill into the soup and serve.

Stuffed Meatball Soup with Rice
[Shusha Kololik]

One of Armenia's most distinguished soups.

Serves 4

1 pound lean lamb or beef,
  ground twice
Salt
¼ cup grated onion
2 teaspoons flour
1 tablespoon milk
1½ teaspoons Cognac
2 tablespoons beaten egg
Freshly ground black
  pepper to taste
2 tablespoons finely
  chopped parsley
4 hard-cooked eggs,
  peeled

3 tablespoons butter
1 small onion, finely
  chopped
8 cups lamb or beef broth,
  salted on the generous
  side
½ cup uncooked long-
  grain white rice
2 tablespoons finely
  chopped fresh tarragon
  or to taste
1 beaten egg (optional)

Salt the meat and pound until pasty. Cover with the grated onion and continue pounding. Sprinkle with the flour, milk, and Cognac. Add the beaten egg and pound until light. Add the pepper and parsley and beat until well blended. Taste for seasoning. Cover and refrigerate 30 minutes. Divide into 4 equal parts. Moisten your hands by dipping them in a bowl of ice water. Roll each part around a hard-cooked egg, making 4 oval rolls. Pat smooth the surface of the rolls with ice water and reserve.

In a small skillet melt the butter over moderate heat. Add the chopped onion and sauté until golden brown, stirring frequently. Remove from the heat and set aside. In a large, heavy pot bring the broth to a boil over high heat. Add the rice, reduce the heat, and cook 10 minutes. Add the meatballs and cook about 10 minutes or until the rice and meatballs are tender. Skim off any foam or scum that rises to the top. Pour the contents of the skillet into the soup. Sprinkle with the tarragon. Stir in the beaten egg, cook a few minutes longer, and serve.

Note: You may cut the meatballs in halves to expose the eggs and serve them on a separate plate with the soup.

• *Variation*
Instead of the whole eggs, the meatballs may be stuffed with a mixture of chopped hard-cooked eggs, chopped salted pistachios, fried minced onion, and salt and pepper.

Stuffed Meatball Soup with Bulghur
[Kololik]

Another exceptional Armenian soup, a meal in itself.

Serves 4
STUFFING

1 tablespoon butter
1 small onion, finely
    chopped
¼ cup dried currants
2 tablespoons chopped
    walnuts or pine nuts

¼ teaspoon cinnamon
Salt and freshly ground
    black pepper to taste

KEYMA (exterior of meatballs)

1 pound lean lamb or beef,
  ground twice
Salt and freshly ground
  black papper to taste

¼ cup fine bulghur,
  washed and drained
1 egg, beaten

SAUTÉED ONION

3 tablespoons butter
1 medium onion, finely
  chopped

TOMATO BROTH

8 cups lamb or beef broth
3 tablespoons tomato paste
Salt
2 medium potatoes,
  peeled and cubed

2 tablespoons finely
  chopped parsley

Make the stuffing: In a small skillet melt the butter over moderate heat. Add the onion and sauté until golden brown, stirring frequently. Add the remaining ingredients and mix well. Remove from the heat and set aside.

Make the *keyma:* Pound the meat until pasty and season with the salt and pepper. Add the bulghur and egg and continue to beat until thoroughly blended. Taste for seasoning. Moisten your hands by dipping them in a bowl of ice water and form the mixture into 1½-inch balls. Stuff each as follows: Indent with your forefinger, pressing gently to make a hollow. Place a spoonful of the stuffing in the opening, and with moistened hands reshape the *keyma* around the stuffing to enclose it securely. Pat smooth the surface of the ball with ice water. Repeat this procedure with the remaining *keyma* and stuffing. Set aside.

Sauté the onion: In a small skillet melt the butter over moderate heat. Add the onion and sauté until richly browned, stirring frequently. Remove from the heat and reserve.

Make the tomato broth: In a large, heavy pot bring the broth and tomato paste to a boil over high heat. Salt on the generous side. Add the potatoes and half of the sautéed onion. Reduce the heat, cover, and cook 10 minutes. Add the stuffed meatballs and cook 20 minutes or until done. Stir in the remaining sautéed onion, sprinkle with the parsley, and serve.

• *Variation*
Instead of the above stuffing, you may use a mixture of chopped dried prunes, chopped walnuts, fried minced onion, and salt and pepper to taste. Another popular stuffing favored by Armenians living in the Caucasus is the native sour plums.

Stuffed Meatball Soup with Saffron
[Kiufta Bozbash]

A sophisticated and elaborate Azerbaidzhani soup, well worth the time and effort it demands.

Serves 4

1 pound lean lamb,
    ground twice
2 tablespoons uncooked
    long- or medium-grain
    white rice
1 medium onion, grated
Salt and freshly ground
    black pepper to taste
As many pitted dried

¼ cup butter
1 large onion, finely
    chopped
⅔ cup drained canned
    chick-peas
¼ teaspoon powdered
    saffron or to taste
    dissolved in 1
    tablespoon warm water

prunes as there are
meatballs
6 cups lamb or beef broth
3 medium potatoes,
peeled and cut in large
chunks

2 finely chopped scallions,
including 2 inches of
the green tops

In a mixing bowl combine the meat, rice, grated onion, and salt and pepper. Knead until well blended. Taste for seasoning. Moisten your hands by dipping them in a bowl of ice water and form the mixture into 1½-inch balls. Stuff each as follows: Indent with your forefinger, pressing gently to make a hollow. Place a prune in the opening, and with moistened hands reshape the meat mixture around the prune to enclose it securely. Pat smooth the surface of the ball with ice water. Repeat this procedure with the remaining meat mixture and prunes. Set aside.

In a large, heavy pot bring the broth to a boil over high heat. Add enough salt to make the broth just slightly over-salted. The salt helps bind the balls together and prevents them from falling apart. Add the meatballs and potatoes to the broth, reduce the heat, and cook 15 minutes.

Meanwhile, in a small skillet melt the butter over moderate heat. Add the onion and sauté until richly browned, stirring frequently. Pour the contents of the skillet into the soup. Add the chick-peas and cook 10 minutes. Stir in the dissolved saffron and pepper to taste and cook 5 minutes. Sprinkle with the scallions and serve.

Note: Azerbaidzhanis stuff the meatballs with the native sour plums when in season. Minced *kyurdyuk* is added with the saffron, and the finished soup is sprinkled with crushed dried mint and served with trimmed scallions and powdered *sumakh* on the side. Some people flavor the broth with peeled, seeded, and finely chopped fresh tomato or a little tomato paste before adding the meatballs and potatoes.

Georgian Meat Soup
[Kharcho]

Serves 4

1 pound boneless lean beef or lamb, cubed

8 cups cold water

⅓ cup uncooked long-grain white rice

2 medium onions, finely chopped

2 large cloves garlic, finely chopped

2 medium tomatoes, peeled, seeded, and finely chopped

Salt and freshly ground black pepper to taste

2 teaspoons wine vinegar or Sour Plum Sauce (page 218) to taste

Finely chopped fresh dill, coriander, or parsley or a combination of parsley, coriander, and mint to taste

Place the meat in a large, heavy pot. Add the water, cover, and simmer 1 hour, skimming off any foam or scum that rises to the surface. Add the rice, onions, garlic, tomatoes, and salt and pepper and cook 30 minutes. Stir in the vinegar, sprinkle with the herbs, and serve.

Note: ¼ pound fresh sour plums may be added with the rice.

Meat and Lentil Soup with Dried Fruits
Armenia
[Vospapour]

Serves 6

1 pound boneless lean
   lamb or beef, cubed
8 cups water
Salt and freshly ground
   black pepper to taste
1 cup dried lentils

2 tablespoons butter
2 medium potatoes,
   peeled and cubed
½ cup dried apricots
½ cup dried pitted prunes
⅓ cup chopped walnuts

In a large, heavy pot combine the meat, water, and salt and pepper. Cover and simmer 1 hour, skimming off any foam or scum that rises to the surface. Stir in the lentils and cook 15 minutes.

Meanwhile, in a heavy skillet heat the butter over moderate heat. Add the potatoes and sauté, turning to brown evenly on all sides. Add to the soup with the fruit and walnuts and additional water if needed. Simmer 30 minutes or until done and serve.

Note: You may use 1 cup dried apricots and omit the prunes. A few tablespoons fresh coriander or tarragon may be stirred into the soup before serving.

Lamb Soup with Coriander and Saffron
[Chikhirtma]

This pleasantly tart soup, which can also be made with chicken, is one of the classics of the Caucasian repertoire.

Serves 4 to 6

¾ pound boneless lean lamb, cut into 1-inch cubes
6 cups water
1 tablespoon butter
1 medium onion, finely chopped
1 tablespoon flour
Pinch powdered saffron dissolved in ¼ cup warm water

Salt and freshly ground black pepper to taste
2 tablespoons white wine vinegar
2 egg yolks
Finely chopped fresh coriander leaves to taste

Combine the lamb and water in a heavy pot. Cover and simmer about 1½ hours or until the meat is very tender. Skim off any foam or scum that rises to the surface.

Meanwhile, in a small skillet melt the butter over moderate heat. Add the onion and sauté until golden, stirring frequently. Sprinkle with the flour and cook, stirring, 1 minute. Stir in a little of the meat stock and blend well. Add the contents of the skillet to the pot containing the lamb and broth and cook 10 minutes. Add the dissolved saffron, salt and pepper, and the vinegar and bring to a boil. Reduce heat to low and keep the soup at a simmer.

In a small bowl beat the egg yolks until frothy. Gradually add a little of the simmering broth, beating constantly. Return the mixture to the pot of broth and simmer a few minutes longer, stirring constantly. Do not allow the soup to boil. Taste for seasoning. Sprinkle with the coriander and serve.

Lamb Soup with Chestnuts, Quince, and Prunes
[Parcha Bozbash]

An outstanding Azerbaidzhani soup that speaks for itself.

Serves 4

1 pound boneless lean
lamb, cut into 1-inch
cubes

Salt and freshly ground
black pepper to taste

3 tablespoons butter

1 medium onion, finely
chopped

4 cups beef broth

1 medium potato, peeled
and cubed

1 small quince, peeled,
cored, and cubed

½ cup dried pitted prunes
or 1 cup fresh sour
prunes

¼ pound chestnuts,
shelled and peeled
(page 167)

⅔ cup drained canned
chick-peas, rinsed

2 tablespoons Clarified
Butter (page 262) or
regular butter

Season the lamb with the salt and pepper. In a heavy pot melt the 3 tablespoons butter over moderate heat. Add the lamb and onion and sauté until browned, stirring frequently. Add the broth and season to taste with salt. Cover and simmer 30 minutes. Add the potato, quince, prunes, and chestnuts. Cover and simmer 20 minutes. Add the chick-peas and simmer, covered, about 15 minutes or until done. Stir in the Clarified Butter and allow it to melt before serving the soup.

Note: ¼ teaspoon ginger or a pinch of powdered saffron dissolved in 2 tablespoons warm water may be added with

the chick-peas and the soup served sprinkled with 1 teaspoon crushed dried mint, accompanied by chopped onion
and *sumakh* on the side. In the Caucasus, ground *kyurdyuk* is normally used instead of the clarified butter, and
dried chick-peas rather than canned ones. The dried chick-
peas are soaked several hours, drained, and added at the
beginning with the broth.

• *Variation*

LAMB SOUP WITH CHESTNUTS, POTATOES, AND PRUNES

(Kavourma Bozbash)

Omit the quince, chick-peas, and the Clarified Butter used
at the end. Use 2 potatoes and ½ pound chestnuts. Just
before serving the soup, stir in a pinch of saffron which
has been dissolved in 2 tablespoons hot water. Season to
taste with freshly ground black pepper and sprinkle with 3
tablespoons minced fresh coriander leaves or parsley. Another variation is to substitute 1 peeled, seeded, and
chopped tomato for the prunes. Omit the saffron.

Dumpling Soup Azerbaidzhan
[Dyushbara]

Variations of this dish, which probably originated in the
East and traveled west with the movement of the nomads,
exist throughout Europe and Asia under different names in
different countries. The stuffed dumplings are certainly
related to the Russian *pelmeny*, Ukrainian *vareniky*, Central Asian *manty*, and Chinese *mant'ou*.

Serves 4

1 recipe Egg Noodle Dough (page 175)	Salt and freshly ground black pepper to taste
½ pound lean ground lamb or beef	2 quarts beef or chicken broth
1 medium onion, grated	1 tablespoon crushed dried mint
¼ cup finely chopped fresh coriander leaves or parsley	Plain or garlic-flavored wine vinegar

Divide the dough into two equal parts, shaping each into a ball. Cover with a kitchen towel and lest rest at room temperature 30 minutes.

Combine the lamb, onion, coriander, and salt and pepper in a bowl. Knead with your hands until well blended and smooth. Taste for seasoning and set aside.

On a lightly floured surface, roll out 1 ball of dough about ¹/₁₆ inch thick. Cut into 1½-inch squares. Place about ½ teaspoon of the meat mixture just above the lower left corner of each square. Moisten the edges of each square with a finger dipped lightly in cold water. Fold the dough over the filling so that each square forms a triangle. Pinch the edges together to seal. Dip your fingers in water and bring the two outer corners of each triangle together, pinching firmly. Repeat with the second ball of dough and the remaining filling.

In a large, heavy pot bring the broth and additional salt to a rolling boil over high heat. Drop the dumplings into the broth. Reduce the heat and cook 7 to 10 minutes or until they rise to the surface. Serve sprinkled with the mint and accompanied by the wine vinegar.

Note: Armenians make a similar soup called *mantabour*. The dumplings are served separately, accompanied by a bowl of Garlic Yogurt Sauce (page 214) to be used as a topping for them.

Chicken Soup with Rice, Chick-Peas, and Prunes Azerbaidzhan

The addition of prunes and dill elevates an ordinary soup from mundane oblivion to gourmet status.

Serves 6

1 2½-pound chicken
6 cups cold water
1 large onion, sliced
Salt and freshly ground
  black pepper to taste
¼ cup butter
1 large onion, finely
  chopped

½ cup uncooked long-
  grain white rice
1 cup drained canned
  chick-peas, rinsed
2 cups dried pitted prunes
½ cup finely chopped
  fresh dill or to taste

Place the chicken in a large, heavy pot and cover with the water. Bring to a boil over high heat. Skim off the foam or scum that rises to the top. Add the sliced onion and salt and pepper. Reduce the heat to low, cover, and simmer 1½ hours or until the chicken is tender. Transfer it to a plate and remove the skin. Cut the meat into slivers and reserve. Strain the stock and set aside.

In a large, heavy saucepan heat the butter over moderate heat. Add the chopped onion and sauté until golden brown, stirring frequently. Pour in the strained stock and the rice and bring to a boil over high heat. Reduce the heat to low, cover, and simmer 15 minutes. Add the chick-peas and prunes and cook 15 minutes. Add the reserved chicken and cook a few minutes more. Taste for seasoning. Sprinkle with the dill and serve.

Note: Fresh sour plums may be substituted for the dried prunes. Some Azerbaidzhanis like to sprinkle the finished soup with crushed dried mint.

- *Variation*

CHICKEN SOUP WITH RICE, CHESTNUTS, AND PRUNES
Add ¼ pound chestnuts, shelled and peeled (page 167), with the prunes and ¼ teaspoon powdered saffron or to taste dissolved in 1 tablespoon warm water with the slivered chicken. Sprinkle the finished soup with minced fresh coriander or parsley rather than the dill. This dish may also be prepared with 1 large peeled, seeded, and chopped tomato, in which case the prunes and saffron are omitted.

Georgian Chicken Soup with Walnuts
[Kharcho]

This soup, with its interesting blend of ingredients and flavors, is uniquely Georgian.

Serves 4

1 2½-pound chicken, cut up
6 cups water
Salt to taste
2 medium onions, finely chopped
3 large tomatoes, peeled, seeded, and mashed
1½ cups shelled walnuts
2 to 3 cloves garlic, crushed

1 teaspoon cinnamon
Freshly ground black pepper to taste
Aromatic peppercorns (page 263) to taste if available
1 bay leaf
3 or 4 sprigs fresh coriander leaves if available

In a large, heavy pot combine the chicken, water, and salt. Bring to a boil over high heat. Skim off the foam or scum that rises to the top. Reduce the heat to low, cover, and simmer 45 minutes. Transfer the chicken to a plate and remove the skin and bones. Shred the meat and return it to the pot. Add the onions and tomatoes, cover, and simmer 20 minutes.

Meanwhile, pound the walnuts to a paste with the garlic. Add the cinnamon, pepper, and aromatic peppercorns and blend well. Stir the mixture into the soup along with the bay leaf, coriander, and salt to taste and simmer 10 minutes. Remove the bay leaf and serve.

Note: Fresh sour plums, stoned and chopped, may be substituted for the tomatoes.

Chilled Fruit Soup

On a hot day what could be more refreshing than this delicate and delicious soup, which can function either as a first course or as a dessert?

Serves 4

½ pound peaches
½ pound tart red plums
½ pound cherries
3 cups water
½ cup sugar or to taste
½ teaspoon cinnamon

1 teaspoon arrowroot dissolved in a little water
Sour cream or whipped cream (optional)

Combine the fruit, water, sugar, and cinnamon in an enameled or stainless steel saucepan. Bring to a boil over high heat, stirring constantly until the sugar dissolves. Reduce the heat and simmer about 15 minutes or until the fruit is tender. Drain, reserving the liquid. Remove the stones and rub the fruit through a fine sieve. Return the puree with the reserved liquid to the pan. Taste and add more sugar if you like. Add the dissolved arrowroot into the hot fruit mixture and bring to a boil, stirring constantly. Simmer until slightly thickened. Remove from the heat and cool. Serve chilled, garnished with the sour cream if desired.

4. EGG DISHES

Eggs play an important role in Caucasian meals and are prepared in many appetizing ways. Fried, scrambled, boiled, poached, baked, or cooked in omelets, they are enhanced with various flavorings, including garlic, onion, tomato, herbs, spices, yogurt, cheese, and even fruits and nuts. Supplemented with bread, a salad, and perhaps yogurt, most Caucasian egg dishes are substantial enough to make a satisfying lunch. Some are equally suitable as a first course or side dish.

The Caucasian omelet is an extremely versatile and flexible creation that lends itself to countless appealing combinations and serves many different purposes. It is firm and thick in texture, with the egg acting as the binding element for the various ingredients it may incorporate. It is usually cooked in butter, preferably Clarified Butter. When done, it is turned onto a serving platter and sliced like a cake. Small pieces may be served as an hors d'oeuvre, while larger portions make an excellent first course, side dish, or main course. Since this type of omelet can be eaten cold as well as hot, it is a great party favorite and popular picnic fare.

Cauliflower Omelet Georgia

Serves 2 to 4

1 medium head
   cauliflower, separated
   into flowerets
5 tablespoons butter
1 large onion, finely
   chopped
2 tablespoons finely
   chopped fresh parsley or
   coriander leaves

4 eggs
Salt
¼ cup finely chopped
   fresh dill

Cook the cauliflower in boiling salted water until half tender. Drain and cool. In a heavy skillet with an ovenproof handle, melt 3 tablespoons of the butter over moderate heat. Add the onion and sauté until soft but not browned, stirring frequently. Add the cauliflower and the remaining 2 tablespoons butter and sauté until the vegetables turn golden brown. Sprinkle with the parsley and mix gently but thoroughly. Beat the eggs with a pinch of salt until frothy, then beat in the dill. Pour over the vegetables. Poke holes in several places to allow the eggs to penetrate downward. Cover and cook over low heat until the eggs set. Or bake in a preheated 425° oven about 5 minutes or until the eggs are just firm. Serve at once.

Mushroom Omelet Azerbaidzhan

Serves 2

2 tablespoons butter
1 small onion, finely
  chopped
¼ pound mushrooms,
  washed, dried, and
  sliced

Salt and freshly ground
  black pepper to taste
4 eggs
2 tablespoons finely
  chopped parsley

In a heavy skillet with an ovenproof handle, melt the butter over moderate heat. Add the onion and mushrooms and sauté until golden brown, stirring frequently. Season with the salt and pepper. Beat the eggs well and pour over the vegetables. Mix gently but thoroughly. Bake in a preheated 425° oven about 5 minutes or until the eggs are just firm. Sprinkle with the parsley, cut into wedges, and serve at once.

Eggplant Omelet Azerbaidzhan

Serves 4

1 small eggplant, peeled
  and cubed
Salt
2 tablespoons butter or
  more

1 medium clove garlic,
  crushed
Freshly ground black
  pepper to taste
4 eggs

1 cup scallions, chopped, including 2 inches of the green tops	2 tablespoons finely chopped fresh mint leaves or parsley
1 medium tomato, peeled, seeded, and chopped	

Sprinkle the eggplant with the salt and let stand 15 minutes. Rinse and dry with paper towels. In a heavy skillet with an ovenproof handle, melt 1 tablespoon of the butter over moderate heat. Add the eggplant and sauté until golden brown on all sides, adding more butter if necessary. Transfer to a plate and keep warm.

Place the remaining 1 tablespoon butter in the skillet and heat. Add the scallions and sauté until soft but not browned, stirring frequently. Add the tomato and garlic, stir, and cook until the tomato juice is absorbed.

Return the eggplant to the skillet and mix gently. Season with salt and pepper. Beat the eggs well with a pinch of salt and pour over the vegetables in the skillet. Bake in a preheated 425° oven about 5 minutes or until the eggs are just firm. Sprinkle with the mint and serve immediately, with a bowl of unflavored yogurt or Garlic Yogurt Sauce (page 214) on the side.

Note: 1 medium minced onion may be substituted for the scallions. The tomato and garlic may be omitted.

Spinach Omelet

Serves 2

1 pound spinach, washed
    and stemmed
4 tablespoons butter
4 scallions, finely
    chopped, including 2
    inches of the green tops
1 medium tomato, peeled,
    seeded, and chopped

Salt and freshly ground
    black pepper to taste
4 eggs
Unflavored yogurt or
    Garlic Yogurt Sauce
    (page 214)

Cook the spinach in lightly salted boiling water for a few minutes. Drain thoroughly and chop coarsely. In a heavy skillet with an ovenproof handle, melt the butter over moderate heat. Add the scallions and sauté until soft but not browned, stirring frequently. Add the tomato and cook a few minutes. Stir in the spinach, season with the salt and pepper, and cook a minute or so longer. Beat the eggs well and pour over the vegetables. Mix gently but thoroughly. Bake in a preheated 425° oven about 5 minutes or until the eggs are just firm. Cut into wedges and serve at once, accompanied by a bowl of the yogurt.

Note: 1 small onion may be substituted for the scallions. Two tablespoons minced fresh herbs (dill, parsley, and coriander) may be stirred into the spinach mixture just before adding the beaten eggs. The tomato may be omitted.

Salami, Green Pepper, and Tomato Omelet

Serves 3

¼ cup butter or olive oil
1 small onion, finely
　chopped
1 large green pepper,
　seeded, deribbed, and
　finely chopped

2 large tomatoes, peeled,
　seeded, and chopped
¼ pound Italian salami,
　finely chopped
6 eggs
Salt to taste

In a heavy skillet with an ovenproof handle, heat the butter over moderate heat. Add the onion and green pepper and sauté until soft but not browned. Add the tomatoes and salami and cook a few minutes. Beat the eggs well with the salt and pour over the contents of the skillet. Mix gently but thoroughly. Bake in a preheated 425° oven about 5 minutes or until the eggs are just firm. Cut into wedges and serve at once.

Eggs with Scallions, Bread, and Cheese

Serves 2

4 tablespoons butter
4 thick slices French
　bread, cubed
8 scallions, chopped,
　including 2 inches of
　the green tops

4 eggs
Salt and freshly ground
　black pepper to taste
⅓ cup freshly grated
　Parmesan, Romano, or
　Gruyère cheese

In a heavy skillet with an ovenproof handle, melt the butter over moderate heat. Add the bread cubes and scallions and sauté until golden brown, stirring frequently. Beat the eggs well with the salt and pepper. Mix in the cheese. Pour over the bread and scallions. Poke holes in several places to allow the egg mixture to penetrate downward. Bake in a preheated 425° oven about 5 minutes or until the eggs are just firm. Serve at once.

Note: Instead of mixing the cheese with the beaten eggs, you may sprinkle it evenly over them just before serving.

Eggs with Bulghur Armenia
[Havgitov Kiufta]

Serves 4

6 tablespoons butter or oil
2 large tomatoes, peeled, seeded, and chopped
⅔ cup fine bulghur
4 eggs
Salt and freshly ground black pepper to taste

4 to 6 scallions, finely chopped, including 2 inches of the green tops
⅔ cup finely chopped parsley or a mixture of parsley and fresh mint leaves or basil

In a small saucepan heat 4 tablespoons of the butter over moderate heat. Add the tomatoes and cook gently until they are sauced, stirring and mashing them frequently with a fork or spoon. Remove from the heat. Add the bulghur, mix well, and set aside about 15 minutes or until the bulghur absorbs the liquid and softens.

Beat the eggs with the salt and pepper until frothy, using a large fork or whisk. In a heavy skillet heat the remaining 2 tablespoons butter over moderate heat. Add the eggs and reduce the heat. When the eggs have set slightly, stir constantly with a fork until thick and creamy. Remove from the heat and cool slightly. Add to the bulghur mixture and mix gently. Season to taste with salt and pepper. Transfer to a serving dish. Sprinkle with the scallions and parsley and serve warm or cold.

Eggs with Fish Azerbaidzhan

Serves 2

4 tablespoons butter
1 medium onion, finely
    chopped
1 pound fish fillets (trout,
    flounder, or other fish)
Salt and freshly ground
    black pepper to taste

¼ cup flour
4 eggs
¼ cup finely chopped
    fresh coriander leaves,
    parsley, or dill

In a small skillet heat 2 tablespoons of the butter over moderate heat. Add the onion and sauté until golden brown, stirring frequently. Remove from the heat and set aside.

Wash the fish under running cold water and dry thoroughly with paper towels. Cut into small serving pieces. Sprinkle with the salt and pepper on both sides. Roll in the flour and fry in the remaining 2 tablespoons butter until golden brown on both sides.

Transfer the fish to an oiled, shallow baking dish. Spread the sautéed onion evenly over and around it. Beat the eggs well with a pinch of salt and pour over the fish. Poke holes in several places to allow the eggs to penetrate downward. Bake in a preheated 425° oven about 5 minutes or until the eggs set. Sprinkle with the coriander and serve at once.

Note: Armenians prepare a similar dish using trout. Instead of the coriander, the finished dish is garnished with fresh tarragon leaves and, sometimes, eggs cooked sunny-side up, which are placed over the fish just before serving.

Ground Meat with Eggs

Serves 2

2 tablespoons butter
1 medium onion, finely chopped
½ pound lean ground lamb or beef
1 small tomato, peeled, seeded, and chopped
2 tablespoons finely chopped parsley

Salt and freshly ground black pepper to taste
4 eggs
⅓ cup freshly grated Parmesan, Romano, or Gruyère cheese

In a heavy skillet with an ovenproof handle, melt the butter over moderate heat. Add the onion and sauté until soft but not browned, stirring frequently. Add the meat and cook until lightly browned, breaking it up with a fork. Add the tomato, parsley, and salt and pepper and cook 10 minutes, stirring frequently. Beat the eggs well with a pinch of salt. Pour over the meat and mix well. Sprinkle the top evenly with the grated cheese. Bake in a preheated 450° oven 8 to 10 minutes or until the eggs are firm.

Note: ¼ teaspoon cinnamon may be added with the tomato.

• *Variation*
Omit the cheese, or stir it into the browned meat mixture. Do not beat the eggs. Make 4 depressions in the meat mixture and break an egg into each one. Sprinkle the eggs with paprika, cover the skillet, and simmer until the eggs set. If omitting the cheese, 1 clove crushed garlic may be added with the onion and the finished dish served with a bowl of unflavored yogurt on the side.

Eggs with Apricots and Walnuts Armenia
[Dziranov yev Ungouyzov Havgit]

Serves 4

1 cup dried apricots, chopped	2 tablespoons butter
3 tablespoons sugar or to taste	¼ cup chopped walnuts
	4 eggs
	Cinnamon to taste

In a small saucepan combine the apricots with water just to cover. Add the sugar and bring to a boil over high heat, stirring constantly to dissolve the sugar. Reduce the heat and cook until the apricots are soft and the liquid in the pan is absorbed. Remove from the heat and set aside.

In a heavy skillet melt the butter over moderate heat. Add the walnuts and sauté until golden brown, stirring frequently. Add the apricots, mix well, and spread in an even layer over the bottom of the skillet. With a large fork or whisk beat the eggs well with the cinnamon and pour over the apricot mixture. Cover and cook gently until the eggs set. Serve at once.

5. FISH

In the Caucasus fish has been highly valued since very ancient times. During the Neolithic Age, fishing was systematically carried on with nets secured in place with stone weights. Today Transcaucasia has a flourishing fishing industry based on the resources of the Black and Caspian seas and Lake Sevan as well as other lakes, rivers, and streams of the area, where numerous hatcheries are situated.

Caucasians enjoy a wide variety of fish, including trout, salmon, carp, barbel, gangfish, pike perch, mullet, sprat, sturgeon, shellfish, and several other species that are unknown elsewhere, such as the *khramuli* or *kogak*, which is about a foot long, white-fleshed, and delicately flavored. Georgians consider it a special treat when simply boiled in spring water and eaten without the addition of any seasoning, a method that allows the flavor of the fish to remain intact.

Of the many kinds of marketable fish in Azerbaidzhan, one of the most valuable is sturgeon, a species that has existed for hundreds of millions of years. Beluga, the white sturgeon of the Black and Caspian seas, the Kura River, and other waters, furnishes caviar of the highest quality, of which Azerbaidzhan produces approximately two hundred tons annually.

Present-day Armenia is a landlocked country, but fresh fish from its lakes, rivers, and streams is served everywhere. Of the various species, trout, historically and gastronomically the most Armenian of fish, is the greatest delicacy of them all. It has been said that to visit Armenia and miss Lake Sevan is to miss Armenia. And it is Lake Sevan that yields trout of unsurpassed delectability. There are several kinds of trout, with some individual fish weighing thirty pounds or more, but the most famous is the *ishkhan,* or "prince," with its silvery scales and reddish-rose flesh.

Fish are sold live, frozen, and salted. Some, among them salmon, carp, and sturgeon, are available smoked. A remarkable variety of ingredients is used in preparing fish, including such unusual ones as coriander, tarragon, walnuts, *lavash,* and fresh and dried fruit. Lemon wedges or pomegranate seeds, tomato slices, pickled cucumbers or fruits, scallions, parsley, tarragon, coriander, and dill are common garnishes for fish, while walnut sauce and pomegranate syrup are favorite accompaniments.

The age-old way of cooking fish over a charcoal or wood fire and serving it with a simple garnish of parsley, scallions, tomatoes, and lemon slices is still one of the highlights of Caucasian gastronomy. Another classic way of preparing fish is combining it with fruit. This might seem an unlikely liaison, but it is in fact an extremely interesting one that has been highly regarded in the Caucasus for many centuries. Today roasted fish with a stuffing of ground walnuts and dried fruit continues to be an Azerbaidzhani favorite featured at banquets and on special occasions. Other popular fish dishes include Fried Fish, Trout with Walnut Sauce, many steamed and baked recipes, and fish pilafs.

Fish on Skewers

This simple and very popular dish usually calls for sturgeon or swordfish, but any firm, white-fleshed fish may be used.

Serves 4

2 pounds firm, white-fleshed fish
Salt
¼ cup sour cream
¼ cup freshly squeezed and strained lemon juice
2 tablespoons butter, melted

1 bunch scallions, finely chopped, including 2 inches of the green tops
¼ cup finely chopped parsley
2 medium tomatoes, cut into eighths
Lemon wedges

Wash the fish well under running cold water and dry thoroughly with paper towels. Skin, bone, and cut the fish into 1½-inch cubes. Sprinkle with the salt. Combine the sour cream and lemon juice and mix well. Coat the fish thoroughly with the mixture. Thread the cubes close together on skewers, leaving a few inches bare at each end. Broil, preferably over a charcoal fire, 3 to 4 inches from the heat, about 10 minutes or until tender, basting occasionally with the melted butter and the remaining sour cream mixture. Turn the skewers frequently to allow the fish to brown evenly on all sides. Serve immediately, sprinkled with the scallions and parsley and garnished with the tomatoes and lemon wedges.

Note: You may omit the sour cream and lemon juice. Simply brush the fish with the melted butter, broil, and serve as above.

• *Variation*
TROUT ON A SPIT
This is another popular Caucasian specialty. Clean 4 medium trout. Cut down through the throat just behind the gills. With a long-handled spoon, scoop out and discard the entrails. Wash the fish inside and out and dry with paper towels. Carefully make several gashes on the outside with a knife. Sprinkle inside and out with salt and freshly ground black pepper to taste. Put long skewers lengthwise through the fish and grill over charcoal, brushing the fish with melted butter and turning from time to time until golden brown and cooked through. Slide the fish off the skewers onto a heated serving platter and pour fresh pomegranate juice over them. Serve garnished with fresh tarragon leaves or parsley.

Fried Fish

A favorite method of cooking fish in the Caucasus is to sauté it and serve with a sauce or lemon wedges.

Wash, clean, and scale the fish. Cut into thick slices and dry thoroughly with paper towels. Season with salt and freshly ground black pepper, dip in beaten egg if you wish, and dredge with flour. Sauté on both sides in butter, preferably Clarified Butter (page 262), until golden brown and cooked through. Transfer to a heated serving platter. Garnish with chopped scallions and parsley or fresh tarragon leaves. Serve with Pomegranate Syrup (page 219) or fried potatoes, cucumber pickles, and lemon wedges.

Stuffed Fillet of Sole Armenia

Serves 4

8 very thin sole fillets of equal size (about 2 pounds)

1 bunch scallions, finely chopped, including 2 inches of the green tops

¼ cup finely chopped parsley

¼ cup finely chopped fresh dill

6 tablespoons melted

butter, preferably Clarified Butter (page 262)

Salt and freshly ground black pepper to taste

2 eggs, beaten

½ cup fine dry bread crumbs

Lemon wedges

Chopped fresh parsley and dill

Wash the fish well under running cold water and dry thoroughly with paper towels. Mix together the scallions, parsley, and dill in a bowl. Divide into 8 equal parts and set aside.

Prepare each fillet as follows: Brush the surface with melted butter. Spread one part of the scallion mixture evenly over it. Sprinkle with the salt and pepper. Roll up and fasten both ends with toothpicks or sew up with strong white thread. Dip in the beaten eggs, roll in the bread crumbs, and fry in the remaining butter until golden brown on both sides and cooked through. Transfer the rolls onto a heated serving platter. Garnish with the lemon wedges and herbs. Serve at once, accompanied by slices of crustless white bread that have been sautéed in butter, fried potatoes, and pickled fruits such as peaches, pears, or grapes.

Note: The scallions may be sautéed in a little butter before mixing with the herbs. The rolls may be fried in olive oil or a mixture of olive oil and butter rather than butter alone.

Fish with Prunes Azerbaidzhan

The plum fruit roll lends a subtle flavor and fragrance as well as a lovely rose color.

Serves 4

1½ pounds trout or red snapper fillets, cut into serving pieces
6 tablespoons butter
1 medium onion, finely chopped
1 cup water
1 cup dried pitted prunes

1 plum fruit roll or *lavashana* (page 265)
Salt to taste
2 tablespoons finely chopped fresh dill
2 tablespoons finely chopped fresh coriander leaves (optional)

Wash the fish well under running cold water and dry thoroughly with paper towels. In a heavy skillet melt 4 tablespoons of the butter over moderate heat. Add the fish fillets and sauté on both sides. Remove to a plate and set aside.

Place the remaining 2 tablespoons butter in the skillet and heat. Add the onion and sauté until golden brown, stirring frequently. Return the sautéed fish to the skillet. Add the water, prunes, fruit roll, and salt. Bring to a boil, cover, and simmer about 20 minutes or until the prunes are tender and the fruit roll has dissolved. Serve sprinkled with the dill and coriander leaves.

Note: Minced fresh savory or ground coriander may be substituted for the above herbs.

Trout with Walnut Sauce

A distinctive and characteristic Georgian dish.

Serves 4

4 trout (8 to 10 inches long), cleaned
Salt to taste
¼ cup wine vinegar
4 scallions, finely chopped, including 2 inches of the green tops

3 tablespoons finely chopped parsley
Walnut Sauce (below)

Wash the fish well under running cold water. Place in a saucepan with water just to cover. Add the salt and vinegar and cook, covered, until the fish are tender. Remove to a plate and let cool (reserve the fish broth). Sprinkle with the scallions and parsley and serve cold with the Walnut Sauce.

WALNUT SAUCE

1 cup shelled walnuts
2 to 4 medium cloves
  garlic
Salt and cayenne to taste
¼ cup grated onion
3 tablespoons wine
  vinegar

1 tablespoon finely
  chopped fresh mint
  leaves
2 tablespoons reserved
  fish broth or as needed

Pound the walnuts to a paste with the garlic and the salt and cayenne. Blend in the onion, vinegar, mint, and about 2 tablespoons of the fish broth or enough to make a thick and creamy sauce. Taste for seasoning, cover, and chill.

Fish with Green Peppers and Tomatoes
Armenia

Serves 6

2 pounds fish, cut into
  thick slices (swordfish,
  red snapper, cod, or any
  firm, white-fleshed fish)
⅓ cup olive oil
  (approximately)
2 large onions, cut
  lengthwise in half and
  thinly sliced
2 medium green peppers,
  seeded, deribbed, and
  thinly sliced

2 to 4 medium cloves
  garlic, crushed
¾ cup finely chopped
  parsley
2 large tomatoes, peeled,
  seeded, and thinly
  sliced
1 tablespoon tomato paste
½ cup water
Salt and freshly ground
  black pepper to taste

Wash the fish well under running cold water and dry thoroughly with paper towels. In a large, heavy skillet heat the oil over moderate heat. Add the fish and sauté until golden brown on both sides. Transfer to a plate and set aside.

Add the onions to the skillet and sauté until soft but not browned, stirring frequently. Add the green peppers and sauté until soft, adding more oil if necessary. Add the garlic and sauté a minute or so. Stir in the parsley, tomatoes, the tomato paste dissolved in the water, and the salt and pepper and bring to a boil. Reduce the heat to low, cover, and simmer 10 minutes. Return the fish to the skillet and baste thoroughly with the sauce. Cover and simmer 15 minutes, adding a little water if necessary. Serve cold, accompanied by crusty bread.

Baked Trout with Tomatoes Armenia

Serves 4

2 pounds trout fillets
Salt to taste
5 tablespoons melted
　butter
1 small onion, sliced ⅛
　inch thick and separated
　into rings
2 medium tomatoes, thinly
　sliced and seeded

2 to 4 large cloves garlic,
　finely chopped
Freshly ground black
　pepper to taste
2 tablespoons finely
　chopped fresh tarragon
　leaves (optional)
¼ cup finely chopped
　parsley (optional)

Wash the fish well under running cold water and dry thoroughly with paper towels. Place skin side down in a shallow baking dish brushed with butter. Sprinkle with the salt and melted butter. Cover with the onion rings, tomato slices, and garlic. Grind the pepper over all. Bake in a preheated 375° oven 20 to 25 minutes or until the fish is tender, occasionally basting with the juices in the pan. Sprinkle with the tarragon and parsley, if desired, and serve.

Note: Whitefish, red snapper, cod, bass, or flounder may also be prepared as above.

Baked Stuffed Fish

This intriguing and time-honored Azerbaidzhani delicacy, which ranks as a classic, is often served at banquets.

Serves 4

4 small carp or bass, about 1½ to 2 pounds each
6 tablespoons butter
1 large onion, finely chopped
1 cup ground walnuts
½ cup dried apricots, chopped
2 to 4 medium cloves garlic, crushed
1 tablespoon Pomegranate Syrup (page 219)
¼ cup milk (approximately)
Salt and freshly ground black pepper to taste
1 egg, beaten
1 cup finely chopped fresh coriander leaves or parsley
½ cup finely chopped scallions, including 2 inches of the green tops
Pickled cucumbers, sliced

Clean and hollow out each fish as follows: Trim off the protruding fins, then snap off the backbone at the base of the tail by bending the tail forward. Using the palms of your hands, roll the fish back and forth on a board to loosen the backbone and the flesh. Cut the fish through the throat behind the gills, leaving the head attached by a hinge of skin. With a long-handled spoon, scoop out the entrails through this opening and discard. Wash the fish thoroughly inside and out with cold water, then pull out the backbone. Beginning from the tail, press the fish gently but firmly with your fingertips, forcing the loosened flesh out of the loosened skin through the opening behind the gills, taking care to keep the skin intact and the head attached. Remove the bones from the fish meat and discard, then place the meat in a sieve and wash under running cold water. Drain and pat the fish meat dry with paper towels, then pass it through a food grinder.

Prepare the stuffing: In a large heavy skillet heat 4 tablespoons of the butter over moderate heat. Add the onion and sauté until golden brown, stirring frequently. Add the walnuts and apricots, reduce the heat to low, and cook 2 or 3 minutes. Remove from the heat and add the ground fish meat, garlic, Pomegranate Syrup, milk, salt and pepper, and the beaten egg. Mix well and cool to room temperature.

Rinse the fish skins under running cold water. Drain and dry thoroughly inside and out with paper towels. Using a long-handled spoon, fill each skin tightly with the stuffing mixture so that the fish skin will form its original shape. Arrange the stuffed fish side by side in an oiled shallow baking dish. Dot with the remaining 2 tablespoons butter. Bake in a preheated 400° oven about 30 minutes or until tender, basting occasionally with the pan juices. Garnish with the coriander leaves, scallions, and pickled cucumbers and serve at once.

6. POULTRY AND GAME

Some of the most glorious dishes of the Caucasian cuisine have been created for poultry and game. Exquisite combinations redolent of herbs and spices and incorporating nuts, vegetables, fruits, and wine blend together to produce incomparable delights.

Among the domestic fowl chicken is the most popular. Once a great delicacy reserved for honored guests and noteworthy events, it has become a plentiful and inexpensive everyday dish that is prepared in numerous imaginative ways. Recipes for turkey, duck, and goose, typical holiday favorites, are also varied and interesting.

Poultry may be served boiled, stewed, roasted, broiled, or fried. Game birds are usually roasted, broiled, or occasionally boiled, in which case they are served chilled. A lean bird is rubbed thoroughly with melted butter or oil before roasting and basted frequently with pan drippings or additional fat as it cooks. The skin of fat duck or goose is pricked around the thighs, back, and lower part of the breast to allow excess fat to escape, and the bird is basted periodically with boiling water during roasting to help dissolve its subcutaneous fat. An interesting Caucasian technique is to brush a chicken with sour cream before frying it. This method results in a moist bird with a rich golden brown color.

A favorite preparation method as ancient as civilization itself is roasting on a spit over charcoal or wood embers. An authentic barbecue feast is certain to include several different kinds of birds. One ancient Armenian recipe specifies no less than a chicken or wild duck, squab, quail, woodcock, plover, teal, partridge, and pheasant—all intended for the same meal!

Chicken on a Spit with Pomegranate Syrup Azerbaidzhan
[Juja Kebab]

The Pomegranate Syrup greatly enhances the taste of the chicken and lends it an exotic character.

Serves 2

1 2-pound chicken, split in half
Salt and freshly ground black pepper to taste
⅓ cup sour cream or as needed
1 small onion, peeled, cut into ⅛-inch-thick slices, and separated into rings

Fresh coriander or parsley sprigs
Pomegranate Syrup (page 219 or lemon wedges

Dry the chicken with paper towels. Rub with the salt and pepper and put on a spit. Brush generously with the sour cream. Broil, preferably over charcoal, turning and brushing frequently with sour cream, about 45 minutes or until the chicken is tender. Remove from the spit and serve, garnished with the onion rings and coriander sprigs and accompanied by the Pomegranate Syrup.

Chicken on a Spit with Sour Plum Sauce
Georgia

The flavor the Sour Plum Sauce imparts to grilled chicken is both excellent and original.

Serves 2

1 2-pound chicken, split in half	¼ cup melted butter or as needed
Salt and freshly ground black pepper to taste	Sour Plum Sauce (page 218)

Dry the chicken with paper towels. Rub with the salt and pepper and put on a spit. Brush well with the butter. Broil, preferably over charcoal, about 45 minutes or until the chicken is tender, turning and brushing frequently with butter. Remove from the spit and serve with the Sour Plum Sauce.

● *Variation* (Armenia)
Omit the Sour Plum Sauce. If desired, brush the chicken with equal amounts of melted butter and fresh strained

lemon juice rather than the butter alone. Broil as above. Serve garnished with fresh or pickled cucumber slices, sliced tomatoes, and parsley sprigs and accompanied by lemon wedges. Partridge and squab are also delicious broiled in this manner.

Pressed Fried Chicken
[Tabaka]

A celebrated Georgian specialty also favored by Armenians.

Serves 2
1 2-pound chicken
Salt and freshly ground
   black pepper to taste

1 clove garlic, crushed
   (optional)
3 tablespoons Clarified
   Butter (page 262)

Dry the chicken with paper towels. Cut it lengthwise in half along the breast without separating it. Beat into a flat form without removing the bones. Rub the chicken thoroughly with the salt and pepper and the garlic. In a heavy skillet heat the butter over moderate heat. Lay the chicken flat, skin side down, in the butter. Lay a heavy weight, such as another skillet laden with a heavy object (5 to 10 pounds), on top of the chicken. Fry about 20 minutes or until a deep golden brown, regulating the heat as necessary to avoid burning. Turn the chicken over and continue to fry, again under the weight, about 20 minutes or until it is nicely browned and cooked through. Serve garnished with fried potatoes, tomato wedges, and fresh or pickled cucumber slices and accompanied by a good tomato sauce, a nut sauce (chap. 13), or a bowl of hot chicken broth flavored with a clove of garlic which has been crushed with salt to taste.

● *Variation*
Flatten the chicken as above and rub with salt. Brush the skin side with sour cream and fry as above. Turn the chicken over, brush with sour cream, and continue frying as directed. Garnish with pickled cucumber slices and serve with a bowl of Sour Plum Sauce (page 218) on the side.

Chicken Stew with Wine
[Chakhokhbili]

Here is another of Georgia's national dishes, famous throughout the Soviet Union. Joseph Stalin, himself a Georgian, was reportedly extremely fond of *chakhokhbili* and also of *shashlik*, which during the Second World War was prepared to such perfection by his Georgian chef that Stalin made him a major general!

Serves 4

1 2½- to 3-pound chicken, cut into serving pieces
3 tablespoons butter
1 medium onion, finely chopped
½ cup chicken broth
½ cup Madeira, port, or sherry
1 bay leaf
Salt and freshly ground black pepper to taste
Lemon slices

| 2 tablespoons tomato paste | Finely chopped parsley or |
| 1 tablespoon wine vinegar | dill |

Dry the chicken thoroughly with paper towels. In a large, heavy skillet melt the butter over moderate heat. Add the chicken pieces, skin side down, and sauté, turning to brown evenly on all sides. Remove to a plate and set aside.

Add the onion to the skillet and cook until golden brown, stirring frequently. Add the chicken broth, tomato paste, vinegar, Madeira, bay leaf, and salt and pepper and bring to a boil. Return the chicken to the skillet, cover, and simmer about 45 minutes or until the chicken is tender, adding a little more broth if necessary. Arrange the chicken on a heated serving dish and put a slice of lemon on each piece. Sprinkle with the parsley and garnish with tomato halves which have been fried in butter. Serve with a Plain Rice Pilaf (page 144 or page 145).

• *Variation*
The fried chicken and onion may be placed in a casserole between layers of peeled and thickly sliced ripe tomatoes, with salt and pepper to taste, and allowed to simmer 1 hour or until the chicken is pink and tender.

Chicken with Peaches Azerbaidzhan

This admirable combination is further enhanced when served over a bed of Plain Bulghur Pilaf.

Serves 4

1 2½- to 3-pound chicken, cut into serving pieces
3 tablespoons butter
Salt and freshly ground black pepper to taste
1 medium onion, finely chopped
Cinnamon

1 cup chicken broth
4 large firm peaches, not quite ripe
Grated rind and juice of 1 lemon
2 tablespoons sugar or to taste

Dry the chicken with paper towels. In a large, heavy casserole melt the butter over moderate heat. Add the chicken, skin side down, and sauté, turning to brown evenly on all sides. Remove to a plate, season with the salt and pepper, and set aside.

Add the onion to the casserole and cook until golden brown, stirring frequently. Add 1 teaspoon cinnamon, the chicken broth, and additional salt and pepper and bring to a boil over high heat. Return the chicken to the casserole and baste it thoroughly with the sauce. Cover and bake in a preheated 350° oven 40 minutes. Peel the peaches, remove the pits, and cut them into thick slices. Arrange them over the chicken. Sprinkle with the lemon rind and juice, the sugar, and, if desired, a little cinnamon. Baste the peaches with the sauce in the casserole, cover, and bake 20 minutes. Serve with Plain Bulghur Pilaf (page 170).

Note: Quinces, tart green apples, or pears may be substituted for the peaches. The fruit slices may be sautéed in a little butter with a sprinkling of cinnamon and sugar before placing them over the chicken.

Chicken with Walnut and Pomegranate Sauce Azerbaidzhan [Fisidzhan]

Late fall is the hunting season for pheasant and wild duck on the shores of the Caspian Sea and an ideal time to make this extraordinary stew, which ranks among the glories of Azerbaidzhani cookery. If you are lucky enough to be able to obtain one of these birds, you can make a truly exotic *fisidzhan;* otherwise you can still create a splendid and authentic *fisidzhan* by using a chicken as suggested below.

Serves 4

1 2½- to 3-pound chicken, cut into small serving pieces
Salt and freshly ground black pepper to taste
4 tablespoons butter
1 medium onion, finely chopped
2 cups ground walnuts
2 cups chicken broth or water

1 cup fresh pomegranate juice or 3 tablespoons Pomegranate Syrup (page 219)
2 to 3 tablespoons freshly squeezed and strained lemon juice or to taste
½ teaspoon cinnamon
Sugar to taste (optional)

Dry the chicken with paper towels. Season with the salt and pepper. In a large, heavy skillet heat the butter over moderate heat. Add the chicken, skin side down, and sauté until nearly tender, turning to brown evenly on all sides. Remove to a plate and set aside.

Add the onion to the skillet and sauté until golden brown, stirring frequently. Add the walnuts and mix thoroughly. Add the chicken broth, pomegranate juice, lemon juice, cinnamon, and additional salt and pepper and stir until well blended. Bring to a boil over high heat, reduce the heat to low, and simmer 10 minutes. Taste for seasoning and add the sugar if needed. Add the sautéed chicken to the skillet and baste with the sauce. Cover and simmer about 30 minutes or until the chicken is tender. Skim as much fat as possible from the surface of the sauce. Serve with Plain Rice Pilaf I (page 144).

Note: This dish may also be prepared with roast or fried duck, cubed lamb, or meatballs.

Roast Chicken with Walnut Sauce
[Kotmis Satsivi]

A Georgian classic that can also be made with turkey.

Serves 4

1 3-pound chicken
4 tablespoons melted butter, preferably Clarified Butter (page 262)

Salt and freshly ground black pepper to taste
Walnut Sauce I (page 215)

Dry the chicken inside and out with paper towels. Brush the cavity and entire surface thoroughly with the butter. Place the chicken on its side on a rack in a shallow roasting pan just large enough to hold it comfortably. Roast in a preheated 450° oven 10 minutes. Turn the chicken to the other side, baste with additional butter, and roast 10 minutes. Turn the bird breast side up, baste again, and season with the salt and pepper. Reduce the heat to 375° and roast the chicken 40 minutes or until done, basting every 10 minutes with the juices in the pan when the butter is used up. Transfer the chicken to a heated serving platter and let stand 5 minutes before carving. Serve with the Walnut Sauce.

Roast Turkey with Fruit and Rice Stuffing
Armenia
[Porov Hintgahav or Amich]

Serves 10

1 7- to 8-pound turkey
Stuffing (below)
8 tablespoons melted
    butter

2 cups hot water
Parsley sprigs

Dry the turkey inside and out with paper towels. Fill the body cavity with the stuffing. Sew the vent with strong white thread and truss the turkey. Brush thoroughly with the melted butter and place breast side up in a shallow roasting pan just large enough to hold the turkey comfortably. Add the hot water to the pan. Place the pan in a preheated 450° oven. Reduce the heat immediately to 325° and bake the bird about 20 minutes per pound or until tender, basting frequently with the remaining butter and the pan juices. When done, remove the turkey to a heated serving platter and remove the trussing strings. Let stand 5 or 10 minutes, then cut into serving pieces. Spoon the pan juices over the turkey, garnish with the parsley sprigs, and serve.

STUFFING

¾ cup blanched almonds

¾ cup dried apricots

¾ cup raisins

8 tablespoons butter

2 cups cooked long-grain
white rice

1 teaspoon cinnamon

½ teaspoon ground cloves

Salt to taste

Sauté the almonds, apricots, and raisins in 4 tablespoons of the butter over low heat, stirring frequently, until the nuts are lightly browned. Remove from the heat. Add the rice, cinnamon, cloves, salt, and the remaining 4 tablespoons butter and mix well.

Note: If you prefer, you may brush the turkey with butter and roast it in the usual manner, basting frequently. If using a meat thermometer, cook to an internal temperature of 190°.

● *Variation*

A chicken may be prepared in the same way. Or stuff the chicken with Bulghur Pilaf with Dried Fruit and Nut Topping (page 173). Mix together the pilaf and topping ingredients before stuffing into the chicken. Another stuffing used for chicken by Caucasian Armenians is Plain Bulghur Pilaf (page 170) prepared with a fried minced onion and dried *kizil* (the native cornelian cherries).

Roast Goose with Apples Armenia

A sumptuous and impressive main course for a special company or holiday dinner.

Serves 6 to 8

1 9- to 10-pound goose
Salt and freshly ground
  black pepper to taste
1 apple, cored and
  quartered
1 large onion, quartered

8 medium green baking
  apples
¼ cup sugar or to taste
Cinnamon
Butter
Parsley

Remove all exposed fat from the goose. Dry the bird thoroughly inside and out with paper towels. Sprinkle the cavity with the salt and pepper and stuff with the quartered apple and onion. Prick the skin around the thighs, back, and lower part of the breast with the prongs of a fork to allow the fat to escape during roasting. Place the goose breast side up on a rack in a large, shallow roasting pan. Roast in a preheated 425° oven 15 minutes. Reduce the heat to 350° and roast about 2 hours and 15 minutes, basting every 15 minutes with 3 to 4 tablespoons boiling water and removing the excess fat with a bulb baster as it accumulates in the pan.

About 1 hour before the end of cooking, core and peel the upper fourth of each baking apple. Place the apples in the pan around the goose. Sprinkle them with the sugar and cinnamon. Put a pat of butter on each apple and bake until the apples are tender but still intact, basting occasionally with the pan juices.

To test whether the bird is done, prick the thigh. If the juices that run out are a pale yellow, the goose is done. If not, cook a little longer, taking care not to overcook; otherwise the meat will dry out.

To serve, transfer the goose to a large heated platter. Scoop out and discard the stuffing. Place the apples around the goose and garnish with the parsley. Tilt the roasting pan and remove any remaining fat, leaving the juices. Pour the pan juices into a warmed sauceboat and serve.

Note: Roast turkey is also excellent served with apples (or quinces). During the last hour of roasting, place the fruit around the turkey, sprinkle with sugar and cinnamon, top with pats of butter, and proceed as above.

Pheasant, Georgian Style

Daring, exotic, and unmistakably Georgian.

Serves 2 or 3

1 pheasant, trussed	½ cup very strong green
24 green walnuts, shelled	tea
and peeled	¼ cup Malmsey wine
Juice of 3 oranges	3 tablespoons butter
Juice of 1½ pounds	Salt and freshly ground
grapes, strained	black pepper to taste

Place the pheasant in a heavy casserole. Add the remaining ingredients, cover, and simmer about 45 minutes or until tender. Serve the pheasant in the sauce.

7. MEAT DISHES

Over the centuries Caucasians have devised numerous splendid ways of preparing meat. Although there are many interesting and unusual recipes for beef, veal, and pork, lamb is by far the favorite meat of the region, and some of the finest lamb dishes in the world are to be found in the Caucasus. Among these the most celebrated is *shashlik*, cubed pieces of meat roasted on a skewer. Less famous and dramatic but equally delicious are the almost unlimited number of stews and casseroles that also use cubed meat. Imaginatively seasoned with herbs and spices and incorporating a rich variety of vegetables, legumes, fruits, and wine, these aromatic, nourishing, and satisfying dishes form the backbone of the Caucasian diet.

Ground meat prepared in enticing ways is another triumph of Caucasian cuisine. Whether broiled, as in Ground Lamb on Skewers (page 121), combined with bulghur, as in Raw Lamb and Wheat Balls (page 25), or used as an ingredient for stuffed vegetables and fruits (see chap. 8), it provides an economical basis for a number of palate-pleasing creations. Recipes for meatballs vary delightfully from place to place, with one extraordinary version calling for one meatball weighing no less than four pounds and enclosing a small whole chicken!

A delicacy much appreciated by Georgians is suckling pig roasted to a crackling brown, while roast baby lamb constitutes a highlight of Armenian cooking, usually reserved for weddings and other notable occasions. There are several interesting methods of preparing it. In the countryside the lamb is placed in a pit over a bed of smoldering charcoal. Then the top is completely covered with earth and the lamb left to roast slowly for several hours. For the ultimate in flavor some Caucasian recipes recommend feeding the lamb with salt 8 to 10 hours before slaughtering it. Another popular way of cooking whole baby lamb is roasting it on a spit. The lamb is seasoned with salt and basted with melted *kyurdyuk* as it cooks until it becomes richly browned and crisp on the outside and succulently tender within. Traditionally roast baby lamb is accompanied by pilaf, fresh vegetables such as tomatoes, green peppers, and scallions, fresh herbs, and *lavash*.

Broiled Skewered Lamb
[Shashlik]

The origin of this most famous of all Caucasian meat dishes is lost in the night of time. Exactly where it had its genesis—in the Caucasus, Central Asia, or the Eastern Mediterranean—is uncertain. What is certain is that *shash-*

lik has been a great favorite throughout this entire area for at least three thousand years and undoubtedly deserves the universal recognition it enjoys.

Shashlik is most commonly made with lamb, preferably tender young lamb, but it can also be made with beef, pork, chicken, fish, venison, wild bear, and kid. Although one can broil the meat in the oven, nothing can equal the taste and aroma of *shashlik* grilled over wood embers or charcoal, particularly if the flames are perfumed with herbs or bunches of grapevines.

The meat of fresh tender young lamb need not be marinated and is delicious grilled on its own. Older lamb or lamb from the shoulder is usually left from several hours to several days in a marinade containing lemon juice, pomegranate juice, or wine vinegar.

Shashlik is excellent presented on a bed of Plain Rice Pilaf. However, in the Caucasus it is often served with a simple garnish of fresh vegetables and herbs: rings of raw onion, small bundles of trimmed scallions, wedges of lemon, slices of cucumber, raw or grilled tomatoes, and sprigs of coriander or parsley. The usual accompaniments to *shashlik* include Pomegranate Syrup (*narsharab*), Sour Plum Sauce (*tkemali*), and dried powdered barberry (*barbaris*) or *sumakh*.

Serves 4

2 pounds boneless leg of
   lamb, trimmed of excess
   fat and cut into 1½- to
   2-inch cubes
1 medium onion, grated
1 teaspoon salt
¼ teaspoon freshly ground
   black pepper
½ cup finely chopped
   parsley (optional)

2 medium onions,
   quartered and separated
4 tablespoons melted
   butter
2 medium tomatoes, cut
   into eighths
2 scallions, trimmed
1 lemon, quartered
Sour Plum Sauce (page
   218)

¼ cup wine vinegar or
    freshly squeezed and
    strained lemon juice

Sumakh (page 266)
    (optional)

Combine the lamb, grated onion, salt, pepper, parsley, and vinegar in a deep bowl. Mix well, cover, and let stand at room temperature 2 to 3 hours or in the refrigerator 5 to 6 hours. Turn the pieces of meat about from time to time to keep them well moistened.

Remove the lamb from the marinade and thread the cubes tightly on long skewers, alternating them with the pieces of onion and leaving a few inches bare at each end. Broil, preferably over charcoal, about 15 minutes or until the lamb is richly browned outside and pink and juicy inside, turning and brushing frequently with the butter.

Using a fork, push the lamb and onions off the skewers onto warmed individual plates. Garnish with the tomatoes, scallions, and lemon. Serve with the Sour Plum Sauce and *sumakh*.

• *Variation*
1 teaspoon dried oregano leaves may be substituted for the parsley. The pieces of onion can be marinated along with the lamb or separately in fresh pomegranate juice before threading them on the skewers. In the Caucasus melted *kyurdyuk* is often used instead of the butter. Or you may omit the butter and substitute 2 tablespoons olive oil and lemon juice for the vinegar.

Note: Another way of serving the *shashlik* is over a platter of Plain Rice Pilaf (page 144 or page 145), garnished with minced scallions and lemon slices, and accompanied by Pomegranate Syrup (page 219).

Broiled Skewered Beef
[Basturma Shashlik]

Serves 4

2 pounds beef fillet or
  boneless sirloin, cut into
  1½-inch cubes
1 medium onion, finely
  grated
¼ cup red wine vinegar or
  fresh pomegranate juice
1 teaspoon salt
¼ teaspoon freshly ground
  black pepper

Melted butter (optional)
2 medium tomatoes, cut in
  eighths
8 scallions, trimmed
Fresh coriander or parsley
  sprigs
1 lemon, quartered
Sumakh (page 266)
  (optional)

In a large bowl combine the meat, onion, vinegar, and salt
and pepper and mix well. Cover and let stand at room temperature 3 hours or in the refrigerator 6 hours, turning the
cubes of meat about in the marinade occasionally to keep
them well moistened.

Remove the meat from the marinade and thread on long
skewers, leaving a few inches bare at each end. If desired,
brush the meat with the butter and broil, preferably over
charcoal, about 15 minutes or until the meat is done to
your taste, turning frequently.

Using a fork, push the meat off the skewers onto warmed
individual plates and garnish with the tomatoes, scallions,
coriander, and lemon. Serve at once, accompanied by the
sumakh.

Note: You may substitute grilled tomatoes for the raw
ones.

Skewered Saddle of Lamb with Kidneys
[Karski Shashlik]

Serves 6

1 saddle of lamb with
kidneys
1 large onion, finely grated
¼ cup wine vinegar
½ cup finely chopped
parsley
1 teaspoon salt
¼ teaspoon freshly ground
black pepper
Melted butter (optional)
12 very small tomatoes

12 scallions, chopped,
including 2 inches of
the green tops
1 small onion, cut into
⅛-inch-thick slices and
separated into rings
(optional)
1 lemon, cut into wedges
Parsley sprigs
Sumakh (page 266)
(optional)

Have the saddle of lamb cut into large pieces, allowing
2 or 3 per serving. In a large bowl combine the lamb with
the onion, vinegar, parsley, salt, and pepper and mix well.
Cover and let stand at room temperature 3 hours or in the
refrigerator 6 hours, turning the meat about in the marinade occasionally to keep it well moistened.

Remove the meat from the marinade and thread on
skewers, leaving a few inches bare at each end. If desired,
brush with the butter and broil over charcoal, turning to
brown on both sides. When the lamb is about half done,
thread the cleaned kidneys and tomatoes on separate
skewers and broil them quickly, turning to brown on all
sides.

To serve, push the lamb, kidneys, and tomatoes into a
heated oval serving platter. Garnish with the scallions,
onion rings, lemon wedges, and parsley. Serve at once
with the *sumakh.*

Note: The *shashlik* may also be served with Sour Plum Sauce (page 218) or Pomegranate Syrup (page 219). In the Caucasus, clarified *kyurdyuk* is sometimes used instead of the butter.

Broiled Skewered Pork with Pomegranate Syrup

The subtle piquancy of the Pomegranate Syrup and the fresh flavors of tomato and scallions provide ideal foils for the crisp cubes of grilled pork in this exceptional Armenian *shashlik*.

Serves 4

1 medium onion, grated
1 tablespoon olive oil
2 tablespoons
   Pomegranate Syrup
   (page 219)
2 teaspoons dried oregano
   or thyme leaves
1½ teaspoons salt
Few grindings black
   pepper

2 pounds boneless lean
   loin of pork, cut into
   1½-inch cubes
2 medium tomatoes, cut
   into eighths
8 scallions, chopped,
   including 2 inches of
   the green tops
Pomegranate Syrup
   (page 219)

Combine the onion, oil, 2 tablespoons Pomegranate Syrup, oregano, salt, and pepper in a deep bowl and mix well. Add the pork and stir until thoroughly coated with the mixture. Cover and let stand at room temperature 3 to 4 hours or in the refrigerator 5 to 6 hours. Turn the pieces of meat about from time to time to keep them well moistened. Remove the pork from the marinade and thread the cubes tightly on long skewers, leaving a few inches bare at each end. Broil, preferably over charcoal, until cooked through and richly browned on all sides, turning frequently.

Using a fork, push the pork off the skewers onto warmed individual plates. Garnish with the tomatoes and scallions. Serve with a bowl of Pomegranate Syrup on the side and accompany with Rice Pilaf with Dried Fruits (page 153) or Flaming Holiday Pilaf (page 155).

Note: The pork may also be marinated, broiled, and served according to the recipe for Broiled Skewered Lamb (page 95).

Broiled Skewered Liver Azerbaidzhan

Serves 4

1 pound calf's or lamb's
   liver, cut into 1½-inch
   squares
¼ pound lamb fat or
   kyurdyuk (page 265),
   cut into small pieces
24 large cherry tomatoes
Lightly salted water
1 small onion or

4 scallions, including 2
   inches of the green tops,
   finely chopped
½ cup finely chopped
   parsley
Sumakh (page 266) or
   lemon wedges
Salt and freshly ground
   black pepper to taste

Thread the liver on long skewers, alternating the pieces with the pieces of lamb fat and leaving a few inches bare at each end. Spear the tomatoes on separate skewers.

Sprinkle the liver with the lightly salted water. Broil the living and tomatoes quickly over charcoal until browned, turning frequently. Take care not to overcook the liver. When done it should be brown on the outside but pink and juicy inside.

Push the meat and tomatoes off the skewers onto heated individual plates and garnish with the onion and parsley. Serve at once with the *sumakh* and salt and pepper.

Note: Omit the broiled tomatoes. Serve the liver with fresh sliced cucumbers and tomatoes.

Broiled Fillet of Beef

Serves 4

4 6-ounce fillet steaks, trimmed of fat and gristle
Salt and freshly ground black pepper to taste
4 scallions, finely

chopped, including 2 inches of the green tops
¼ cup finely chopped fresh coriander leaves or parsley
1 lemon, sliced

Place the steaks between sheets of waxed paper and pound slightly. Sprinkle with the salt and pepper and broil to taste, preferably over charcoal. Take care not to overcook the steaks. They should be browned on the outside but still pink and juicy inside. Place on warmed individual serving plates. Sprinkle with the scallions and coriander and garnish with the lemon slices. Serve at once, accompanied by sautéed potatoes and a green vegetable.

Roast Lamb Shoulder with Liver and Rice Stuffing Armenia
[Grpanouk]

It does take a little time to prepare this dish, but in the end the effort proves worthwhile.

Serves 6

4 tablespoons butter
½ pound lamb's liver
1 cup uncooked long-grain white rice
¼ cup slivered blanched almonds
¼ cup dried currants
½ teaspoon ground cardamom
2 cups lamb or beef broth, salted to taste

1 3- to 4-pound boned lamb shoulder, trimmed of excess fat and with a pocket for stuffing
Salt and freshly ground black pepper to taste
1½ cups water
Fresh dill

In a small skillet melt 1 tablespoon of the butter over moderate heat. Add the liver and sauté briefly until no longer pink. Remove from the heat, cut into very small pieces, and set aside.

In a heavy saucepan melt the remaining 3 tablespoons butter. Add the rice and sauté a minute or two, stirring constantly. Add the almonds, currants, cardamom, sautéed liver, and broth and bring to a boil over high heat while you stir. Reduce the heat to low, cover, and simmer until all the liquid in the pan is absorbed and the rice is tender.

Sprinkle the lamb lightly inside and out with the salt and pepper. Fill the pocket with as much of the rice mixture as it will hold, reserving the remainder in the saucepan. Sew the opening with a large needle and strong white thread. Place fat side up on a rack in a roasting pan and insert a meat thermometer into the thickest part of the meat. Add the water to the pan and bake in a preheated 350° oven until the thermometer registers 160° to 170°, depending on how well done you like the meat to be.

When done, transfer the lamb to a large, warmed serving platter and let stand 10 minutes before carving. Serve garnished with the dill. Reheat the reserved pilaf with a tablespoon or two of hot water to moisten. Fluff with a fork and simmer until heated through. Serve in a separate dish for second helpings, accompanied by a bowl of chopped fresh dill.

• *Variation*
4 lamb kidneys may be substituted for the liver, or ¼ pound each liver and kidneys may be used. Wash, remove the tough white center from the kidneys, and boil in hot water 3 to 4 minutes. Drain and cut into small pieces before frying.

Stuffed Breast of Veal

Serves 4

1 2-pound breast of veal, with a pocket for stuffing

Salt to taste

4 tablespoons butter

½ cup uncooked long-grain white rice

1 cup hot water

½ medium green pepper, seeded, deribbed, and finely chopped

1 small onion, finely chopped

¼ cup finely chopped fresh dill

1 egg

¼ cup seedless golden raisins, washed and drained

½ teaspoon cinnamon

¼ teaspoon ground cloves

Freshly ground black pepper to taste

½ cup canned tomato sauce

Wipe the meat with a damp cloth. Sprinkle lightly inside and out with the salt.

Prepare the stuffing: In a small saucepan melt 2 tablespoons of the butter over moderate heat. Add the rice and sauté a minute or so until the grains are coated with the butter, stirring constantly. Add the water and bring to a boil. Reduce the heat to low, cover, and simmer undisturbed until the liquid in the pan is absorbed and the rice is tender but still somewhat firm, not mushy. Remove from the heat and let cool.

In a small skillet heat the remaining 2 tablespoons butter over moderate heat. Add the green pepper and onion and sauté until golden brown, stirring frequently. Remove from the heat. Combine with the rice. Add the dill, egg, raisins, cinnamon, cloves, additional salt, and pepper. Mix gently but thoroughly, taking care not to mash or break the rice.

Stuff the breast of veal loosely with the rice mixture and sew up the opening with a large needle and strong white thread. Place the stuffed veal in a greased roasting pan. With the tip of a pointed knife, make several incisions in the top of the meat and pour the tomato sauce over. Cover the pan with aluminum foil and bake in a preheated 350° oven 45 minutes. Remove the foil and bake 15 to 30 minutes or until the meat is tender.

Transfer the veal to a heated serving platter and let stand 5 minutes before carving. Remove the strings and spoon out the stuffing into a heated serving bowl. Slice the meat and serve with the stuffing.

Rolled Veal Scallops with Almond Stuffing
Armenia

Serves 4

8 veal scallops
Salt to taste
4 tablespoons butter
2 medium onions, finely
  chopped
⅓ cup finely chopped or
  ground almonds
½ teaspoon paprika

Chicken or beef broth,
  salted to taste
1 large tomato, peeled,
  seeded, and finely
  chopped, or 1 to
  2 tablespoons tomato
  paste dissolved in a
  little of the broth

Place the veal scallops between sheets of waxed paper and pound them very thin. Sprinkle lightly with salt and set aside.

In a heavy skillet melt the butter over moderate heat.

Add the onions and sauté until golden brown, stirring frequently. Remove from the heat, add the almonds, paprika, and additional salt, and mix until well blended. Divide into 8 equal parts. Lay the veal scallops on a large plate. Spread one part of the almond mixture evenly over the entire surface of each scallop. Roll up tightly and pin with a toothpick, or tie securely with string. Arrange the stuffed rolls in a large, heavy skillet. Pour in just enough broth barely to cover them. Add the tomato and bring to a boil over high heat. Reduce the heat to low, cover, and simmer about 20 minutes or until the meat is tender. Remove the toothpicks or string.

Serve with sautéed potatoes or carrots which have been boiled in water until nearly tender, then sliced and sautéed in butter until golden brown on both sides.

Note: Thin slices of lean, tender lamb may be substituted for the veal.

• *Variations*

You may brown the stuffed rolls in 4 tablespoons Clarified Butter (page 262) or a mixture of 2 tablespoons each butter and vegetable or olive oil before adding the broth and tomato. Or transfer the sautéed rolls to a platter. Pour off most of the fat from the pan. Add the tomato and cook 2 minutes. Add ⅔ cup dry white wine and boil 5 minutes. Return the rolls to the pan, cover, and simmer 20 minutes, turning the rolls after 10 minutes.

This dish is also good prepared without the tomato. Sauté the stuffed rolls as above and transfer to a platter. Discard most of the fat from the pan. Pour in ⅔ cup dry white wine and boil 5 minutes, stirring and scraping any brown bits that cling to the pan. Add ½ cup broth and bring it to a simmer. Return the veal to the pan, cover, and simmer 20 minutes.

Roast Suckling Pig Georgia

Serves 8

1 ready-to-cook suckling pig (10 to 12 pounds)

Salt and freshly ground black pepper

¾ cup vegetable oil, olive oil, or melter butter (approximately)

1 small shiny red apple

2 red cherries

Fresh coriander or parsley

Whole medium tomatoes

Wash the pig well inside and out under running cold water and pat it thoroughly dry with paper towels. Rub the abdominal cavity and skin with the salt and pepper. Place a wooden block or a ball of aluminum foil in the pig's mouth to keep it open during cooking. Cover the ears and tail with foil to prevent burning.

Place the pig in a kneeling position on a rack set in a large, shallow roasting pan. Brush it generously all over with the oil. Roast the pig in a preheated 325° oven about 25 minutes per pound, or until brown and crisp on the outside and tender on the inside, basting occasionally with the oil.

When done, transfer the pig to a large, heated platter. Remove the foil from the ears and tail. Remove the wooden block or ball of foil from the mouth and replace it with the apple. Insert a cherry in each eye socket. Garnish the platter with the coriander and surround the pig with the tomatoes.

Note: Spiced fruit such as pears, peaches, and apricots may be substituted for the tomatoes. Suckling pig is especially delicious when roasted on a spit over charcoal.

Pork with Quince

Although the familiar combination of pork and apple is admirable, perhaps even more interesting is that of pork and quince.

Serves 4

1 pound pork tenderloin, sliced ¾ inch thick and pounded ¼ inch thick
Salt and freshly ground black pepper to taste
Flour
4 tablespoons butter, preferably Clarified

Butter (page 262), or as needed
1 lemon, quartered
Sautéed potatoes
Sautéed Quinces (page 203) or Quince Compote (page 241)

Season the pork slices with the salt and pepper. Dip them in the flour and shake off the excess. In a heavy skillet melt the butter over moderate heat. Add the pork slices, a few at a time, and sauté until golden brown on both sides. Transfer to a heated serving platter and serve with the lemon wedges, sautéed potatoes, and Sautéed Quinces or Quince Compote.

Fillet of Beef with Wine Georgia

Serves 4

3 tablespoons butter
1 medium onion, finely chopped

½ cup dry red or white wine
½ cup Salted Cucumbers

1 pound fillet of beef, trimmed of fat and gristle and cut into 1-inch pieces
Salt and freshly ground black pepper to taste
2 tablespoons tomato paste
⅓ cup beef broth
(page 208) or half-sour pickles (sold in jars in Jewish delicatessens), sliced
1 to 2 medium cloves garlic, crushed
2 tablespoons finely chopped parsley

In a heavy saucepan melt 2 tablespoons of the butter over moderate heat. Add the onion and sauté until golden. Add the remaining 1 tablespoon butter to the saucepan and heat. Season the beef with the salt and pepper, add it to the saucepan, and sauté, turning to brown on all sides. Dissolve the tomato paste in the broth and add to the meat. Stir in the wine, Salted Cucumbers, and garlic. Cover and simmer 30 to 40 minutes or until the meat is tender, adding a little more broth if necessary. Serve sprinkled with the parsley.

Note: 1 tablespoon capers may be added with the cucumbers.

Lamb Stew with Wine Georgia [Chakhokhbili]

Serves 4
3 tablespoons butter
1 pound boneless lean lamb, cut into 1-inch cubes
½ cup beef broth
Salt and freshly ground black pepper to taste
¼ cup dry white wine

1 large onion, chopped   ¼ cup finely chopped
2 medium tomatoes,   fresh coriander leaves or
   peeled, seeded, and   parsley
   chopped

In a heavy saucepan melt the butter over moderate heat. Add the lamb and onion and sauté until the lamb is browned on all sides, stirring frequently. Add the tomatoes, broth, and salt and pepper and bring to a boil over high heat. Reduce the heat to low, cover, and simmer 45 minutes. Add the wine and simmer 15 minutes or until the lamb is tender. Sprinkle with the coriander and serve with a Plain Rice Pilaf (page 144 or 145).

• *Variation*
Use 4 medium tomatoes. Omit the broth and wine. Add 1 to 2 cloves crushed garlic with the tomatoes. Beef may be substituted for the lamb.
   For Chicken *Chakhokhbili* consult page 85.

Casserole of Lamb with Vegetables and Fruit
[Ghazan Kyapap]

This artful and delicately aromatic combination will delight even the most sophisticated of palates.

Serves 4
4 medium tomatoes,   thinly sliced
   peeled, seeded, and   1 medium onion, cut

lengthwise in half and
thinly sliced
1 small green pepper,
seeded, deribbed, and
thinly sliced
12 pitted dried prunes
1 pound boneless lean
lamb, cut into 1-inch
cubes

Cinnamon
Ground cloves
Salt and freshly ground
black pepper to taste
Freshly squeezed and
strained juice of 2
lemons
4 tablespoons butter
1 medium eggplant

Spread half the tomato slices in a heavy casserole, then follow with layers of the onion, green pepper, prunes, lamb, and the remaining tomato slices, sprinkling each layer lightly with the cinnamon, cloves, and salt and pepper. Add the lemon juice and dot the surface with the butter. Bring to a boil over high heat. Reduce the heat to low, cover, and simmer 1 hour.

Meanwhile, prepare and fry the eggplant as directed in the recipe for Fried Eggplant with Walnut Sauce (page 191), using approximately ¼ cup vegetable oil.

Add the eggplant to the casserole, cover, and simmer 15 minutes. Serve with a Plain Rice Pilaf (page 144 or page 145), Saffron Rice Pilaf (page 145), or crusty bread.

Note: Dried apricots may be substituted for the prunes and ½ cup fresh pomegranate juice for the lemon juice. In the Caucasus *kyurdyuk* is sometimes substituted for the butter. Thick slices of unpeeled quince or tart apple (or both) which have been sautéed in butter may be added with the eggplant or in place of it.

Lamb with Greens Azerbaidzhan
[Sabza Kavourma]

Serves 4

3 tablespoons butter
1 pound boneless lean
   lamb, cut into 1-inch
   cubes
1 medium onion, finely
   chopped
Salt and freshly ground
   black pepper to taste
¼ teaspoon powdered
   saffron or to taste,
   dissolved in ¼ cup hot
   water
Freshly squeezed and

strained juice of 1 lemon
   or more
1 cup beef broth or water
2 to 3 cups chopped
   spinach leaves
1 cup finely chopped
   scallions, including 2
   inches of the green tops
1 cup chopped fresh
   coriander leaves or
   parsley
¼ cup finely chopped
   fresh dill

In a heavy saucepan melt the butter over moderate heat. Add the lamb and onion and sauté until the lamb is lightly browned on all sides, stirring frequently. Add the salt and pepper, the dissolved saffron, lemon juice, and broth and bring to a boil over high heat. Reduce the heat to low, cover, and simmer about 1 hour or until the lamb is tender, adding more broth if necessary. Stir in the spinach, scallions, and coriander and cook 5 minutes. Sprinkle with the dill and serve with Saffron Rice Pilaf (page 145).

Note: In the Caucasus juice from unripe grapes (*abgora*) is sometimes used instead of the lemon juice. Chopped chives or ½ cup each scallions and chives may be substituted for the scallions.

Lamb with Okra Armenia
[Geragour Pamyayov]

Serves 4

4 tablespoons butter
1 pound boneless lean
    lamb, cut into 1-inch
    cubes
2 medium onions, finely
    chopped
4 medium ripe tomatoes,
    peeled, seeded, and
    chopped
2 cups water or beef broth
Salt and freshly ground
    black pepper or cayenne
    to taste

1 pound tender okra,
    washed and trimmed of
    stem ends, or 2
    10-ounce packages
    frozen okra, defrosted
2 green peppers, seeded,
    deribbed, and diced
Freshly squeezed and
    strained juice of 1 or 2
    lemons

In a heavy saucepan melt the butter over moderate heat. Add the lamb and onion and sauté until the lamb is lightly browned on all sides, stirring frequently. Add the tomatoes, water, and salt and pepper. Bring to a boil over high heat. Reduce the heat to low, cover, and simmer 45 minutes. Add the okra, green peppers, and lemon juice. Cover and simmer 30 minutes or until the lamb and okra are tender, adding more water if necessary. Serve with a Plain Rice Pilaf (page 144 or page 145).

Note: Minced fresh basil to taste may be added with the okra.

Lamb with Eggplant Azerbaidzhan

Serves 4

5 tablespoons butter,
  preferably Clarified
  Butter (page 262)
  (approximately)
1 pound boneless lean
  lamb, cut into 1-inch
  cubes
1 medium onion, finely
  chopped
Freshly squeezed and
  strained juice of 1 lemon
  or to taste

1 cup beef broth
Pinch saffron dissolved in
  ¼ cup hot water
¼ to ½ teaspoon cinnamon
Salt and freshly ground
  black pepper to taste
2 small eggplants
1 medium clove garlic,
  crushed
¼ cup finely chopped
  parsley

In a heavy saucepan melt 2 tablespoons of the butter over moderate heat. Add the lamb and onion and sauté until the lamb is lightly browned on all sides, stirring frequently. Add the lemon juice, broth, the dissolved saffron, cinnamon, and salt and pepper and bring to a boil over high heat. Reduce the heat to low, cover, and simmer 45 minutes or until the meat is tender, adding more broth if necessary.

Meanwhile, remove the stems and hulls from the eggplants. Peel and cut into cubes. Sprinkle generously with salt and let stand 20 minutes. Rinse, squeeze out excess moisture, and dry thoroughly with paper towels. In a heavy skillet melt the remaining 3 tablespoons butter over moderate heat. Add the eggplant cubes and fry until golden brown on all sides, adding more butter if necessary. Add the fried eggplant and garlic to the stew and mix. Taste for seasoning and simmer 10 minutes. Sprinkle with the parsley and serve with a Plain Rice Pilaf (page 144 or page 145).

Note: 1 large tomato, peeled, seeded, and finely chopped, may be added with the broth.

Lamb with Carrots and Onion Armenia

A robust and highly aromatic stew.

Serves 4

5 tablespoons butter
1 pound boneless lean
  lamb, cut into 1-inch
  cubes
1 teaspoon ground cumin
  or to taste
1 tablespoon tomato paste
1 cup dry white wine

Salt and freshly ground
  black pepper to taste
2 large carrots, scraped
  and cut crosswise into
  ¼-inch-thick slices
1 large onion, cut
  lengthwise in half and
  sliced

In a heavy saucepan melt 2 tablespoons of the butter over moderate heat. Add the lamb and sauté until browned on all sides, stirring frequently. Add the cumin, tomato paste, wine, and salt and pepper and mix well. Bring to a boil, reduce the heat to low, cover, and simmer 45 minutes.

Meanwhile, in a heavy skillet heat the remaining 3 tablespoons butter over moderate heat. Add the carrots and onion and sauté until lightly browned, stirring frequently. Add to the lamb, cover, and simmer 30 minutes or until the lamb and vegetables are tender, adding a little water if necessary. Serve with a Plain Rice Pilaf (page 144 or page 145) or Plain Bulghur Pilaf (page 170) or fried potatoes and a green salad.

Lamb with Apples

A sensitively seasoned stew with an exquisite taste and fragrance.

Serves 4

6 tablespoons butter	Salt and freshly ground
1 pound boneless lean	black pepper to taste
lamb, cut into 1-inch	2 cups water or beef broth
cubes	4 medium tart apples
1 medium onion, finely	2 to 3 tablespoons freshly
chopped	squeezed and strained
1 teaspoon cinnamon	lemon juice

In a heavy saucepan melt 3 tablespoons of the butter over moderate heat. Add the lamb and onion and sauté until the lamb is browned on all sides, stirring frequently. Sprinkle with the cinnamon and salt and pepper. Add the water and bring to a boil. Reduce the heat to low, cover, and simmer about 1 hour or until the lamb is tender, adding more water if necessary.

Meanwhile, peel, core, and slice the apples. In a heavy skillet, heat the remaining 3 tablespoons butter over moderate heat. Add the apples and sauté gently until lightly browned on all sides. Add to the lamb with the lemon juice. Simmer 5 minutes. Serve with a Plain Rice Pilaf (page 144 or page 145).

Lamb with Prunes Azerbaidzhan
[Tourshou Kavourma]

Serves 4

3 tablespoons butter
1 pound boneless lean
    lamb, cut into 1-inch
    cubes
1 medium onion, finely
    chopped
Salt and freshly ground
    black pepper to taste

2 cups beef broth
1 cup pitted dried prunes
¼ cup finely chopped
    fresh herbs (dill, mint,
    and coriander leaves or
    parsley)

In a heavy saucepan melt the butter over moderate heat. Add the lamb and onion and sauté until the lamb is lightly browned on all sides, stirring frequently. Add the salt and pepper and broth and bring to a boil over high heat. Reduce the heat to low, cover, and simmer 40 minutes. Stir in the prunes and simmer 20 minutes or until the lamb and prunes are tender, adding more broth if necessary. Sprinkle with the herbs and serve with a Plain Rice Pilaf (page 144 or page 145).

Note: ½ teaspoon cinnamon, ¼ teaspoon nutmeg, and the juice of 1 lemon may be added with the seasonings. Peeled, small, raw potatoes are sometimes added during the last 30 minutes of cooking.

- *Variation*

LAMB WITH PRUNES AND CURRANTS (Shirin Kavourma)

Substitute ½ cup dried pitted prunes and ¾ cup dried currants for the prunes. Stir in ¼ teaspoon powdered saffron dissolved in ¼ cup hot water and simmer as above until done. Omit sprinkling with the herbs.

Lamb with Pumpkin, Prunes, and Beans
[Bouglama]

This dish, with its subtle blending of color, flavor, and bouquet, is a tribute to the culinary talents of the Azerbaidzhanis.

Serves 4

3 tablespoons butter
1 pound boneless lean
    lamb, cut into 1-inch
    cubes
1 medium onion, finely
    chopped
Salt to taste
2 cups beef broth
1 pound pumpkin, peeled
    and cut into 1-inch
    squares
½ cup dried pitted prunes

1½ tablespoons sugar or to
    taste
⅔ cup drained and rinsed
    canned white beans
¼ cup finely chopped
    fresh coriander leaves or
    parsley
¼ cup finely chopped
    fresh dill
Cinnamon
Freshly ground black
    pepper

In a heavy saucepan melt the butter over moderate heat. Add the lamb and onion and sauté until browned on all sides, stirring frequently. Add the salt and broth and bring to a boil. Reduce the heat to low, cover, and simmer 30 minutes. Stir in the pumpkin, prunes, and sugar. Cover and simmer 20 minutes. Add the beans and simmer, covered, 10 minutes. Serve sprinkled with the coriander and dill and accompanied by the cinnamon and pepper.

Lamb with Bread Armenia
[Kalajosh]

Simple to make and flavorful, this is a rustic dish of peasant origin and a countryside favorite.

Serves 4

6 tablespoons olive oil
1 pound boneless lean
  lamb, cut into ½-inch
  cubes
1 medium onion, finely
  chopped
1 large clove garlic,
  crushed

Salt and freshly ground
  black pepper to taste
8 thick slices French
  bread, cubed
Unflavored yogurt

In a heavy saucepan heat 4 tablespoons of the oil. Add the lamb and onion and fry gently until the lamb is tender, stirring frequently. Add the garlic and salt and pepper and cook a few minutes, stirring. Add the bread cubes and the remaining 2 tablespoons oil and cook until the cubes are golden brown, stirring frequently. Serve with the yogurt.

Ground Lamb on Skewers
[Lyulya Kebab]

One of the highlights of Caucasian cuisine, *Lyulya Kebab* is a classic, easy, and delicious way of preparing ground meat and an ideal dish for an outdoor barbecue or picnic.

Serves 4

2 pounds lean lamb, ground twice
2 medium onions, grated
⅔ cup finely chopped parsley
½ teaspoon oregano (optional)
Salt and freshly ground black pepper to taste
Thinly sliced onion rings
Whole small tomatoes broiled on skewers
Scallions, trimmed
Lemon wedges
Parsley sprigs, preferably the flat-leaf variety known as Italian parsley
Sumakh (page 266) or fresh or dried powdered barberry (*barbaris*, page 263) (optional)
Lavash (page 221)

In a large mixing bowl combine the lamb, onions, parsley, oregano, and salt and pepper. Pound or knead until the mixture is well blended and very smooth. Taste for seasoning. With hands dipped in cold water, form portions of the meat mixture into long sausage shapes and thread lengthwise on skewers. (Ideally, the skewers used for *Lyulya Kebab* should be flat-edged and a bit wider than those used for *shashlik*.) Broil the kebabs, preferably over charcoal, 10 to 15 minutes or to taste, turning the skewers frequently so the meat browns evenly on all sides.

Using a fork, push the kebabs off the skewers onto warmed individual plates. Garnish with the onion rings, tomatoes, scallions, lemon wedges, and parsley and serve with the *sumakh* and *lavash*. Or line the plates with *lavash* and serve the kebabs nestling in the bread.

Note: In the Caucasus the lamb is ground with a little *kyurdyuk* before combining it with the other ingredients.

Fried Lamb Patties Azerbaidzhan
[Altya Kiufta]

Serves 4

1 pound lean lamb,
   ground twice
1 medium onion, grated
1 egg yolk
Salt and freshly ground
   black pepper to taste
¼ cup flour
1 large egg, beaten
Fine bread crumbs

2 tablespoons Clarified
   Butter (page 262) or 1
   tablespoon each
   vegetable oil and butter
Cucumber slices
Lemon slices
Thinly sliced onion rings
Finely chopped parsley

Combine the lamb, onion, egg yolk, and salt and pepper in a mixing bowl and knead until thoroughly blended and smooth. Taste for seasoning. With hands moistened in cold water, shape the mixture into flat round patties about 2 inches in diameter. Roll lightly in the flour, dip in the beaten egg, then roll in the bread crumbs.

In a heavy skillet heat the butter over moderate heat. Add the meat patties and fry until evenly browned on both sides, adding more butter if needed. Transfer to a heated serving platter and garnish with the cucumber and lemon slices and the onion rings. Sprinkle with the parsley and serve.

Note: Instead of the above garnish you may serve the fried patties with a bowl of Cinnamon Yogurt Sauce (page 214). Or sprinkle them with minced parsley and onion, garnish with fried or grilled tomato halves, and serve with *sumakh* if you wish.

● *Variations*
Combine the lamb with the onion, 1 egg, 2 slices bread, trimmed of crusts, dipped in water, squeezed dry, and crumbled, 1 clove garlic, crushed, ½ teaspoon each cinnamon and oregano, and salt and pepper to taste. Knead and shape the mixture into patties. Roll in toasted, fine bread crumbs and sauté as above. Serve with fried potatoes and a green salad.

LAMB PATTIES IN TOMATO SAUCE (Riza Kiufta)
Prepare the fried lamb patties as described above. In a heavy skillet melt 2 tablespoons butter over moderate heat. Add 1 minced onion and sauté until golden brown, stirring frequently. Add 2 tablespoons tomato paste, 1 cup beef broth, 1 tablespoon freshly squeezed and strained lemon juice or wine vinegar, 2 tablespoons sugar, and salt and pepper and bring to a boil. Lower the heat and simmer until the sauce is reduced. Add the lamb patties, baste with the sauce, and simmer 10 minutes. Sprinkle with 2 to 4 tablespoons each minced fresh dill and coriander or parsley. Serve with a Plain Rice Pilaf (page 144 or page 145) or Plain Bulghur Pilaf (page 170) or mashed potatoes and a green salad.

Festive Meat Rolls

These make a handsome first course and are equally effective on a buffet table.

Serves 4

1 pound lean lamb,
   ground twice
1 medium onion, grated
1 medium clove garlic,
   crushed
3 tablespoons plus ¾ cup
   fine, dry bread crumbs
½ teaspoon curry powder
⅛ teaspoon cinnamon
⅛ teaspoon nutmeg
1 tablespoon finely
   chopped parsley

Salt and freshly ground
   black pepper to taste
4 eggs
1 tablespoon butter
1 beaten egg
3 tablespoons Clarified
   Butter (page 262) or
   olive oil
½ cup dry white wine or
   tomato juice
¼ cup beef broth

Combine the lamb, onion, garlic, 3 tablespoons bread crumbs, curry powder, cinnamon, nutmeg, parsley, and salt and pepper in a deep bowl and knead until thoroughly blended. Taste for seasoning. Divide into 4 equal parts. Form each part into a rectangle about ¾ inch thick. Make a plain omelet with the eggs and 1 tablespoon butter. Divide the omelet into 4 equal parts. Top each rectangle of meat with a slice of the omelet, which has been cut to cover the surface of the meat, and roll up like a jelly roll. Pinch the ends of the roll together to seal. Repeat the shaping and rolling procedure with the remaining 3 parts. With hands moistened in cold water, smooth the surface of the rolls. Dip in the beaten egg, then roll in the remaining ¾ cup bread crumbs.

    In a large, heavy skillet heat the Clarified Butter over moderate heat. Add the meat rolls and fry, turning them to brown evenly on all sides. Transfer the rolls to a platter. Pour off the excess fat from the skillet. Pour in the wine and boil a few minutes. Add the broth and bring it to a simmer. Return the meat rolls to the skillet, cover, and simmer about 30 minutes or until they are done, adding a little more broth if necessary. Serve the rolls hot, accompanied by a Plain Rice Pilaf (page 144 or page 145) or sautéed or mashed potatoes and a green salad. Or cool the rolls, slice thinly, and arrange on a serving platter. Garnish with parsley or coriander leaves and serve as an appetizer or a cold main course.

8. STUFFED VEGETABLES AND FRUITS

Stuffed vegetables and fruits, known as *dolma,* constitute a delightful feature of Caucasian, particularly Armenian and Azerbaidzhani, cooking, covering a wide range of foods both hot and cold. *Dolmas* may be prepared with or without meat. Meat *dolmas* are usually served hot as main dishes, while meatless ones are served cold as appetizers.

Whether these intriguing and exotic creations originated in the Caucasus or in the Middle East is a matter of conjecture. However, they unquestionably enjoy a great popularity throughout the whole region and exist in numerous variations. But few equal the delicacies described in this chapter. Once again the subtlety and originality of Caucasian cuisine, as reflected in the exquisite and ingenious combination of ingredients chosen for each particular *dolma,* set these stuffed vegetables and fruits apart from all others.

Cabbage Leaves Stuffed with Meat and Rice Armenia
[Gaghampov Dolma]

Fragrant herbs and fruits impart flavor and a bouquet of great subtlety to this exceptional *dolma*.

Serves 4

1 pound lean ground lamb
½ cup uncooked long-grain white rice, washed and drained
1 medium onion, grated
¼ cup finely chopped fresh herbs (a mixture of basil, coriander, marjoram, mint, and savory)
Salt and freshly ground black pepper to taste

1 medium-size head white cabbage
½ cup dried apricots, chopped
1 small quince or tart apple, peeled, cored, and chopped
Thin onion rings
3 tablespoons butter
Hot beef broth or water

Combine the lamb, rice, onion, herbs, and salt and pepper in a bowl. Knead thoroughly until the mixture is well blended and smooth. Taste for seasoning and set aside.

Remove the thick core from the cabbage, loosening the leaves without detaching them. Drop the cabbage into a large pot of boiling salted water and boil 6 to 7 minutes or until the leaves are softened. Transfer the cabbage to a plate. Using a long fork, loosen the outer leaves and remove them, being careful not to break them. Place the leaves in a colander to drain and cool. Return the cabbage to the boiling water, cook a few minutes more, and again remove the softened outer leaves. Continue this process until you come to the heart of the cabbage. Reserve the inner leaves. Stuff each of the remaining leaves as follows: Remove the hard rib end and spread the leaf on a plate, cut end toward you. Place about 1 tablespoon (more for larger leaves) of the meat mixture near the cut end. Fold over the sides to enclose the stuffing securely. Beginning at the cut end, roll the leaf firmly away from you toward the tip, forming a cylinder.

Cover the bottom of a heavy casserole with the reserved inner leaves to prevent the stuffed leaves from burning during cooking. Layer the stuffed leaves, seam sides down and close together, in neat rows over them, scattering the apricots, quince, and onion rings between and around the stuffed leaves. Sprinkle with additional salt and dot with the butter. Gently place an inverted plate over the top to keep the stuffed leaves in place while cooking. Add enough broth to reach the plate. Bring to a boil and cover. Reduce the heat and simmer about 1 hour or until tender, adding more broth if necessary. To serve, carefully transfer the stuffed leaves to a heated serving dish and serve them with the pan juices.

Note: You may place the stuffed leaves over a layer of meat bones, then cook them as above. One half cup tomato sauce or the juice of 1 lemon may be added with the broth.

• *Variation*
CABBAGE LEAVES STUFFED WITH MEAT AND BULGHUR
Prepare, stuff, and cook the cabbage leaves as above, using the ingredients given for Grapevine Leaves Stuffed with Meat and Bulghur (page 133).

Cabbage Leaves Stuffed with Chestnuts, Meat, and Rice

Chestnuts and chick-peas, two Azerbaidzhani favorites, lend interest to an unusual recipe.

Serves 4

¼ pound chestnuts, shelled and peeled (page 167)
1 pound lean ground lamb
¼ cup uncooked long-grain white rice, washed and drained
1 medium onion, finely chopped
⅓ cup drained canned chick-peas, shelled
½ cup dried currants
¾ cup finely chopped

fresh coriander leaves or parsley
Salt and freshly ground black pepper to taste
1 medium-size head white cabbage
Freshly squeezed and strained juice of 1 lemon or to taste
1 tablespoon sugar
Beef broth
Cinnamon

In a small saucepan cover the chestnuts with lightly salted boiling water and boil 15 minutes. Drain and chop them.

Place the lamb, chestnuts, rice, onion, chick-peas, currants, coriander, and salt and pepper in a bowl. Mix thoroughly, taste for seasoning, and set aside.

Prepare the cabbage and stuff it with the meat mixture as directed in the recipe for Cabbage Leaves Stuffed with Meat and Rice (above). Cover the bottom of a heavy casserole with the reserved inner cabbage leaves to prevent the stuffed leaves from burning during cooking. Layer the stuffed leaves, seam sides down and close together, in neat rows over them. Sprinkle with additional salt, the lemon juice, and sugar. Gently place an inverted plate over the top to keep the stuffed leaves in place while cooking. Add enough broth to reach the plate. Bring to a boil and cover. Reduce the heat and simmer about 1 hour or until tender, adding more broth if necessary. Sprinkle with the cinnamon and serve the stuffed leaves with their sauce.

Note: ¼ teaspoon saffron dissolved in 1 tablespoon hot water may be added to the broth before pouring it over the stuffed leaves. In the Caucasus a little minced *kyurdyuk* is mixed with the lean lamb. Also, instead of the lemon juice, a mixture of concentrated grape juice (*doshab*) and wine vinegar is added to the broth 20 minutes or so before the end of the cooking period.

• *Variation*
1 small peeled, seeded, and chopped tomato may be added with the broth. Omit the sugar and cinnamon. Serve the stuffed leaves sprinkled with minced fresh dill and coriander or parsley.

Cucumbers Stuffed with Meat and Rice
[Khyar Dolmasi]

An original and immensely satisfying Azerbaidzhani specialty.

Serves 4

⅓ cup uncooked long-grain white rice	1 medium onion, finely chopped
1 pound lean ground lamb	Salt and freshly ground

black pepper to taste
4 large cucumbers
¼ cup all-purpose flour
4 tablespoons Clarified
    Butter (page 262) or 2
    tablespoons each butter
    and vegetable oil

2 tablespoons butter
½ cup finely chopped
    fresh dill or to taste
Cinnamon Yogurt Sauce
    (page 214)
2 medium tomatoes, sliced

Soak the rice in a bowl of boiling salted water 30 minutes. Drain. Combine the lamb, rice, onion, and salt and pepper in a bowl. Knead thoroughly until the mixture is well blended and smooth. Taste for seasoning.

Halve the cucumbers. Using an apple corer, scoop out the seeds of each cucumber and discard, leaving a ¼- to ⅜-inch-thick shell all around. Spoon the meat mixture into the cucumbers. Roll them in the flour, shaking off the excess.

In a large heavy skillet heat the Clarified Butter over moderate heat. Add the cucumbers and sauté, turning to brown lightly on all sides. Arrange them side by side in a buttered shallow baking dish just large enough to hold them comfortably in one layer. Dot with the 2 tablespoons butter. Bake in a preheated 350° oven about 45 minutes or until tender, turning them occasionally and basting with the butter in the pan.

Carefully transfer the stuffed cucumbers to a heated serving platter. Sprinkle with the dill. Serve with the Cinnamon Yogurt Sauce and the sliced tomatoes.

Grapevine Leaves Stuffed with Meat and Rice Azerbaidzhan
[Yarpag Dolmasi]

A widely appreciated dish, perfumed with herbs and spiced with cinnamon.

Serves 6 to 8

1 pound lean ground lamb
1 large onion, finely
   chopped or grated
⅓ to ½ cup uncooked
   long-grain white rice,
   washed and drained
½ cup fresh peas or
   defrosted frozen peas
⅓ cup finely chopped
   fresh dill
⅓ cup finely chopped
   fresh coriander leaves
Salt and freshly ground
   black pepper to taste

1 16-ounce jar preserved
   grapevine leaves or
   about 60 fresh grapevine
   leaves
Chicken or beef broth
1 tablespoon crushed
   dried mint
Cinnamon to taste
Unflavored yogurt or
   Garlic Yogurt Sauce
   (page 214)

Combine the lamb, onion, rice, peas, dill, coriander, and salt and pepper in a bowl. Mix together gently but thoroughly. Taste for seasoning.

Prepare and stuff the grapevine leaves according to the directions given in the recipe for Grapevine Leaves Stuffed with Lentils and Bulghur (page 23), using 1 tablespoon of the meat mixture (or a little more or less, depending on the size of the leaf) for each leaf.

Cover the bottom of a heavy casserole with 10 of the leaves to prevent the stuffed leaves from burning during cooking. Layer the stuffed leaves, seam sides down and close together, in neat rows in the casserole. Sprinkle with additional salt. Gently place an inverted plate over the top to keep them in place while they cook. Add enough of the broth to reach the plate. Bring to a boil and cover. Lower the heat and simmer 50 to 60 minutes, adding a little more hot broth if necessary. Sprinkle with the dried mint and cinnamon. Serve with the pan juices and a bowl of the yogurt.

Note: Azerbaidzhanis living in the Caucasus grind the lean lamb with a little *kyurdyuk*. You may omit sprinkling the vine leaves with the cinnamon and serve them instead with Cinnamon Yogurt Sauce (page 214).

● *Variation* (Armenia)
GRAPEVINE LEAVES STUFFED WITH MEAT AND BULGHUR
Combine 1 pound ground lamb, 1 cup coarse bulghur, 1 medium onion, minced, 3 tablespoons minced green pepper, 2 tablespoons fresh basil or ½ teaspoon dried basil, ⅓ cup tomato juice, ¼ cup tomato paste, and salt and pepper to taste in a bowl. Knead thoroughly until the mixture is well blended and smooth. Stuff the grapevine leaves with the mixture and arrange them in the casserole as above. Cover them with 2 large tomatoes, peeled, seeded, and chopped. Sprinkle with the juice of 1 or 2 lemons, freshly squeezed and strained, and salt to taste. Place an inverted plate over the top and proceed as above. Serve with the pan juices. Cabbage leaves may also be prepared according to this recipe.

Onions Stuffed with Meat and Rice
Azerbaidzhan
[Sogan Dolmasi]

Serves 4

4 large onions, or as many
  as needed
1 pound lean ground lamb
1 cup finely chopped
  onion
¼ cup uncooked long-
  grain white rice, washed
  and drained
¼ cup finely chopped
  fresh dill

¼ cup finely chopped
  fresh coriander leaves
Salt and freshly ground
  black pepper to taste
2 cups beef broth
Cinnamon Yogurt Sauce
  (page 214)

Make a lengthwise slit on one side of each peeled onion, cutting all the way to the center. Cook the onions in boiling salted water about 5 minutes or until soft enough for the layers to be separated. As each layer becomes softened, gently loosen it with a fork, being careful not to break it, and remove it to a colander to drain and cool.

Combine the lamb, chopped onion, rice, dill, coriander, and salt and pepper in a bowl. Knead thoroughly until the mixture is well blended and smooth. Taste for seasoning.

Place 1 tablespoon of the meat mixture on each layer of onion (or more or less, depending on its size) and roll firmly, following its natural curl to form an oval.

Cover the bottom of a heavy casserole with any leftover pieces of onion. Layer the stuffed onions close together in neat rows over them. Pour in the broth and sprinkle with additional salt. Cover and simmer about 40 minutes or until done. Serve the stuffed onions with the pan juices and accompanied by a bowl of the Cinnamon Yogurt Sauce.

Note: In the Caucasus a little *kyurdyuk* is ground with the lean meat. The chopped onion may be sautéed in butter before mixing it with the stuffing ingredients. More rice may be used.

Zucchini Stuffed with Meat and Rice

Quince is the surprising ingredient that gives this *dolma* its special delight.

Serves 4

1 pound lean ground lamb
½ cup uncooked long-grain white rice, washed and drained
1 medium onion, grated
¼ cup finely chopped fresh herbs (a mixture of basil, coriander, marjoram, mint, and savory)
¼ cup beef broth
Salt and freshly ground black pepper to taste

6 medium zucchini (7 by 2 inches each), or as many as needed
1 large quince, peeled, cored, and chopped
Freshly squeezed and strained juice of 1 or 2 lemons or limes
1½ cups water or beef broth
3 tablespoons butter

Combine the lamb, rice, onion, herbs, ¼ cup broth, and salt and pepper in a bowl. Knead thoroughly until the mixture is well blended and smooth. Taste for seasoning.

Cut about ½ inch off the stem ends of the zucchini. Shape into corklike lids and set aside. These will later serve as covers.

Using a squash corer (or an apple corer), scoop out the

pulp of each zucchini and discard (or reserve for some other use), leaving a ¼-inch-thick shell all around. Drop the cored zucchini into a large bowl of salted water and let them soak about 5 minutes. Drain thoroughly. Spoon the stuffing into the zucchini. Cover with the lids.

In a heavy casserole just large enough to hold the zucchini comfortably, place a layer of quince. Arrange the stuffed zucchini side by side over the quince. Cover with the remaining quince. Add the lemon juice, sprinkle with additional salt, and pour in the water. Dot with the butter. Bring to a boil, reduce the heat, cover, and simmer about 1 hour or until tender, adding more hot water if necessary.

Carefully transfer the zucchini to a heated serving platter and serve them with the pan juices.

Note: 1 large egg may be substituted for the ¼ cup beef broth. Parsley may be used instead of the above herbs. An alternate flavoring is ½ teaspoon cinnamon. One quarter-pound dried apricot halves, which have been soaked in cold water to cover and drained, may be substituted for the quince. Use the apricot water for the water called for in the recipe.

• *Variation*
Use a tomato flavoring instead of the quince or apricots. Arrange the stuffed zucchini in the casserole. Dot with 2 tablespoons butter. Dilute 2 tablespoons tomato paste in 1½ cups beef broth. Add the freshly squeezed and strained juice of 1 lemon or to taste and season with salt and pepper. Pour over the zucchini and cook as above. Serve the zucchini sprinkled with minced parsley and accompanied by a bowl of Garlic Yogurt Sauce (page 214). (For this variation use a mixture of fresh dill, coriander or parsley, and basil for the stuffing.)

Apples and Quinces Stuffed with Meat and Rice
[Ashtarak Dolma]

This artful combination is much esteemed by Caucasian Armenians.

Serves 4

1 pound lean ground lamb
1 medium onion, finely chopped
⅓ cup uncooked long-grain white rice, washed and drained
¼ cup finely chopped fresh herbs (coriander, marjoram, savory, and mint or tarragon)
Salt and freshly ground black pepper to taste

4 medium tart eating apples
4 medium quinces
⅓ cup dried apricots
⅓ cup pitted dried prunes
3 tablespoons sugar or to taste
4 tablespoons butter
2 cups beef broth
¼ cup finely chopped parsley

Combine the meat, onion, rice, herbs, and salt and pepper in a bowl. Knead thoroughly until the mixture is well blended and smooth. Taste for seasoning.

Cut about ½ inch off the stem ends of the apples and quinces and reserve. These will later be used as lids. Scoop out the cores to within ½ inch of the bottoms and remove some of the pulp, leaving a ⅓- to ½-inch-thick shell all around.

Spoon the meat mixture into the fruit shells. Cover with the reserved tops. Arrange them side by side in a heavy pan. Scatter the dried apricots and prunes around the stuffed fruits. Sprinkle with the sugar and dot with the butter. Pour the broth into the pan. Cover and simmer about 50 minutes or until the apples and quinces are tender but still intact, not mushy. If necessary a little more broth may be added. Carefully transfer the *dolmas* to a heated serving platter. Sprinkle with the parsley and serve with the pan juices.

Note: The scooped-out fruit pulp may be chopped and added to the pan with the broth.

Quinces Stuffed with Meat and Chestnuts
Azerbaidzhan

A delicately contrived, dill-scented creation.

Serves 4

¼ pound shelled and peeled chestnuts (page 167)
1 pound lean ground lamb
⅔ cup finely chopped fresh dill

Salt to taste
8 medium quinces
1½ tablespoons sugar
4 tablespoons butter
2 cups beef broth

In a small saucepan cover the chestnuts with lightly salted boiling water and boil 15 minutes. Drain and chop them. Place the lamb, chestnuts, dill, and salt in a bowl. Knead until the mixture is well blended. Taste for seasoning.

Cut about ½ inch off the stem ends of the quinces and reserve. These will later be used as lids. Scoop out the cores to within ½ inch of the bottoms and remove some of the pulp, leaving a ⅓- to ½-inch-thick shell all around.

Spoon the meat mixture into the quince shells. Cover with the reserved tops. Arrange them side by side in a heavy casserole. Sprinkle with the sugar and dot with the butter. Pour the broth into the casserole. Cover and simmer 50 to 60 minutes or until the quinces are tender. If necessary more broth may be added. Carefully transfer the *dolmas* to a heated serving platter. Serve with the pan juices.

Note: The scooped-out quince pulp may be chopped and added to the pan with the broth.

• *Variation*
An Armenian stuffing consists of 1 pound lean ground lamb, ¼ cup uncooked long-grain white rice, washed and drained, 1 small minced onion, minced fresh coriander, and salt and pepper to taste. The quinces are stuffed and cooked as above. They are sprinkled with minced parsley just before serving.

Echmiadzin Dolma

This unique dish comes from the town of Echmiadzin, seat of the Armenian Church since the beginning of the fourth century A.D.

Serves 4

1 pound lean ground lamb
½ cup uncooked long-grain white rice, washed and drained
1 medium onion, grated
¼ cup finely chopped fresh herbs (a mixture of basil, coriander, marjoram, savory, and mint or tarragon)
⅓ cup tomato juice (optional)

Salt and freshly ground black pepper to taste
4 baby eggplants
4 small green peppers
4 small firm tomatoes
1 medium quince or tart apple, peeled, cored, and chopped
1½ cups water or beef broth
3 tablespoons butter

Combine the lamb, rice, onion, herbs, tomato juice, and salt and pepper in a bowl. Knead thoroughly until the mixture is well blended and smooth. Taste for seasoning.

Prepare the vegetables for stuffing: Cut about ½ inch off the stem ends of the eggplants. Shape these into corklike lids and set aside. Using a squash corer (or an apple corer), scoop out the pulp of each eggplant and discard, leaving a ¼-inch-thick shell all around. Cut about ½ inch off the stem ends of the green peppers and set aside. Remove the seeds and white membranes. Cut almost through the stem ends of the tomatoes, leaving them attached at one side. Using a spoon, scoop out the insides of each tomato and reserve for some other use, leaving a ¼-inch-thick shell all around.

Spoon the meat mixture into the vegetable shells and cover them with their lids. Arrange them side by side in a heavy casserole just large enough to hold them comfortably. Place the chopped quince between and around the vegetables. Sprinkle with additional salt and pour in the water. Dot with the butter. Bring to a boil, reduce the heat, cover, and simmer about 40 minutes or until tender, adding more hot water if necessary. Carefully transfer the vegetables to a heated serving platter. Serve with the pan juices.

9. PILAFS

Pilaf, known as *plov* or *plav*, has been a basic dish in Caucasian cuisine for centuries. The original pilaf was probably made with wheat, a staple food of the area since earliest recorded history. Today a pilaf of cracked wheat (bulghur) continues to be favored in the mountainous regions of the Caucasus where rice will not grow. However, as one moves east toward the Caspian Sea, rice supplants wheat and gradually comes to dominate the menu as a principal dish and main attraction at banquets.

Although there is an abundance of outstanding rice dishes in Armenia, Azerbaidzhan is even more famous for the excellence and variety of its pilafs. There are scores of Azerbaidzhani pilafs, ranging from plain pilafs that serve as bases or accompaniments for meats and stews to luxurious ones meant to function as main courses and incorporating numerous ingredients such as meat, poultry, fish, vegetables, herbs, eggs, fruits, and nuts.

Caucasian cooks are past masters at preparing rice that is fluffy and flavorful, with each grain dry and separate. There are basically two ways of making rice. In the first, more classic, method (see page 144), the rice is cooked in boiling salted water until half tender. It is then drained immediately, combined with melted Clarified Butter, and cooked over a low flame, without the addition of any water, until done and a crisp, golden-brown crust has formed at the bottom of the pan. When ready to serve, the rice is spooned in a mound on a platter. The crust, which is considered a delicacy, is removed and pieces of it are arranged around the edge of the platter or over the mounded rice to be offered first to guests as triumphant proof of the cook's expertise. Other delectable crusts can be made by lining the bottom of the pan before adding the rice with a thin round layer of unleavened dough known as *kazmag* (page 146), *lavash* (page 221), thin potato slices, or a mixture of parboiled rice, sautéed onion, and eggs.

In the second and simpler method (see page 145), the rice is cooked in water with salt and Clarified Butter until the water is absorbed. It is then sprinkled with additional melted butter and cooked further over low heat. The amount of water needed varies slightly according to the type of rice used, but generally twice as much water is required as the amount of rice to be cooked.

In the following recipes it is best to use long-grain white rice because of its particular ability to remain firm and separate when cooked. In Azerbaidzhan, where several kinds of rice are cultivated, the ones known as *sadri, ambarbi,* and *akilchiki* are used for pilafs prepared according to the first method described above, while *akula* and *chilyali* rices are used for the second and in the preparation of stuffings for various fish, fowl, and meat dishes as well as *dolmas* (page 126).

Caucasians wash the rice thoroughly and soak it in salted water several hours or overnight before cooking it, a step usually unnecessary with American long-grain rice. However, if you are using an imported rice or one that is covered with talc, it is best to rinse it thoroughly under running water until the water runs clear; otherwise the cooked rice will have an undesirably gummy consistency.

After you have sampled some of the recipes in this chapter, you will then realize why these pilafs occupy such a prominent position in Caucasian cuisine and indeed rank among the best and most original rice and wheat dishes in the world.

Plain Rice Pilaf I

Serves 4

8 cups water
1½ tablespoons salt
1½ cups uncooked long-
    grain white rice

4 tablespoons butter,
    preferably Clarified
    Butter (page 262)

In a large pot bring the water and salt to a boil over high heat. Add the rice in a slow stream so as not to disturb the boiling. Boil vigorously, uncovered, 10 minutes. Carefully stir the rice with a spoon 2 or 3 times during cooking. Drain well. Rinse with lukewarm water and drain again.

Melt 2 tablespoons of the butter in a heavy saucepan. Add a few tablespoons of the parboiled rice. Mix it gently with the butter and spread it evenly over the bottom of the pan, being careful not to break or mash the rice. Melt the remaining 2 tablespoons butter. Add the rest of the rice and sprinkle it evenly with the butter. Place a kitchen towel over the pan. Put the lid on and bring the corners of the towel over it. Fasten them there to keep them away from the flame. The cloth will absorb the steam as it rises from the rice, leaving the grains dry and separate. Simmer over low heat 30 to 40 minutes.

Spoon the rice in a mound on a heated serving platter. The bottom layer of rice will form a golden brown and crisp crust. With a metal spatula scrape it out and arrange small pieces around the edge of the platter or over the mounded rice.

Note: Some people use more butter, 6 to 8 tablespoons, for this amount of rice. Chicken or meat broth is sometimes substituted for the water.

• *Variation*
SAFFRON RICE PILAF
Mix the parboiled rice gently but thoroughly with ¼ teaspoon powdered saffron dissolved in 1 tablespoon warm water, then combine it with the melted butter in the saucepan as directed above.

Plain Rice Pilaf II

Serves 4
2½ cups water
1½ teaspoons salt
4 tablespoons butter,
  preferably Clarified
  Butter (page 262)

1½ cups uncooked long-
  grain white rice

In a heavy saucepan bring the water, salt, and 2 tablespoons of the butter to a boil over high heat. Add the rice and boil vigorously for a minute or so. Reduce the heat to low, cover the pan tightly, and simmer undisturbed about 15 minutes or until the liquid in the pan is absorbed. Melt the remaining butter and pour it evenly over the rice. Cover and simmer over very low heat about 30 minutes.

Note: Chicken or meat broth is sometimes substituted for the water.

Rice Pilaf with Kazmag Azerbaidzhan

In this recipe the rice is cooked on a *kazmag*, a thin round layer of dough made with egg.

Serves 4

1 egg
Salt
¾ cup all-purpose flour
　(approximately)
8 cups water
1½ cups uncooked long-
　grain white rice

1 teaspoon vegetable oil or
　Clarified Butter (page
　262)
4 tablespoons melted
　butter, preferably
　Clarified Butter

Prepare the *kazmag*. Beat the egg with a pinch of salt until frothy. Add ½ cup of the flour and blend well. Add about ¼ cup more flour, a tablespoon at a time, until you have a dough that does not stick to the fingers. On a lightly floured board roll out the dough very thinly. Cut a circle to fit the bottom of a heavy casserole which will be used for cooking the rice. Set the *kazmag* aside.

Combine the water and 1½ tablespoons salt in a large pot and bring to a boil over high heat. Add the rice in a slow stream so as not to disturb the boiling. Boil vigorously, uncovered, 10 minutes. Carefully stir the rice with a spoon 2 or 3 times during cooking. Drain well.

Brush the bottom of the casserole with the oil and line it with the *kazmag*. Coat the *kazmag* generously with some of the melted butter. Add the rice and sprinkle evenly with the rest of the butter. Place a kitchen towel over the casserole. Put the lid on and bring the corners of the towel over it. Fasten them there to keep them away from the flame. The cloth will absorb the steam as it rises from the rice, leaving the grains dry and separate. Simmer over low heat about 40 minutes.

Spoon the rice onto a heated serving platter and garnish with wedges of the *kazmag* crust, which will have become golden brown and crisp.

Note: Chicken or meat broth may be substituted for the water. A pinch of saffron is sometimes beaten with the egg and salt when preparing the *kazmag*, before adding the flour.

• *Variation*
SAFFRON RICE PILAF WITH KAZMAG
Before placing the parboiled rice over the *kazmag*, mix it gently but thoroughly with ¼ teaspoon powdered saffron dissolved in 1 tablespoon warm water.

Rice Pilaf with Fried Onion and Egg Crust
Armenia
[Chlav]

A delightful pilaf with an unusual and flavorful crust.

Serves 4

8 cups water
Salt
1½ cups uncooked long-
  grain white rice
8 tablespoons butter,

preferably Clarified
Butter (page 262)
1 medium onion, finely
  chopped
2 eggs

In a large pot bring the water and 1½ tablespoons salt to a boil over high heat. Add the rice in a slow stream so as not to disturb the boiling. Boil vigorously, uncovered, 10 minutes, stirring the rice 2 or 3 times during cooking. Drain thoroughly.

Place 4 tablespoons of the butter in a heavy saucepan and heat over moderate heat. Add the onion and sauté until golden brown, stirring frequently. Sprinkle with about ½ cup of the parboiled rice and mix well. Beat the eggs with a pinch of salt until frothy and pour into the saucepan. Cook over very low heat 4 or 5 minutes, stirring constantly. Add the remaining rice and with a spoon smooth it to the edges of the pan. Melt the remaining 4 tablespoons butter and sprinkle it evenly over the rice. Place a kitchen towel over the pan. Put the lid on and bring the corners of the towel over it. Fasten them there to keep them away from the flame. The cloth will absorb the steam as it rises from the rice, leaving the grains dry and separate. Simmer over low heat about 30 minutes.

Spoon the rice in a mound on a heated serving platter. Arrange small pieces of the brown crust that has formed in the bottom of the pan around the edge of the platter or over the mounded rice.

Rice Pilaf with Dill Azerbaidzhan

Traditional with fried fish, but a superb partner for roast lamb or fowl as well.

Serves 4
Wash 1 large bunch fresh dill in cold water. Plunge it into boiling water. Cover and cook 1 minute. Drain thoroughly. Mince and set aside.

Prepare 1 recipe Plain Rice Pilaf I (page 144), but before steaming the parboiled rice with the butter, mix it with the dill.

Note: You may prepare the rice according to the recipe for Rice Pilaf with Kazmag (page 146), mixing the parboiled rice with the dill before steaming it. Serve the pilaf garnished with wedges of *kazmag* crust.

• *Variation*
RICE PILAF WITH DILL AND OMELET (Shuyyud Plov)
Prepare the rice according to the recipe for Plain Rice Pilaf I (page 144) or Plain Rice Pilaf II (page 145), adding the dill to the saucepan with the rice. While the rice is cooking, make a firm omelet using 2 large eggs, 2 tablespoons milk or cream, ¼ teaspoon salt, and 1 tablespoon butter. Roll the omelet like a pancake and cut it into thin strips. Mound the rice on a heated serving platter. Garnish with the omelet strips, sprinkle with melted butter, and serve.

Rice Pilaf with Omelet Azerbaidzhan
[Plov Shashandaz]

Serves 4

2 tablespoons butter
1 small onion, finely
  chopped
1 tablespoon freshly
  squeezed and strained
  lemon juice
1 teaspoon sugar or to
  taste

4 eggs
Salt to taste
1 recipe Saffron Rice Pilaf
  (page 145)
Melted butter to taste
Cinnamon

In a heavy skillet melt the butter over moderate heat. Add the onion and sauté until golden brown, stirring frequently. Add the lemon juice and sugar and mix well. In a small bowl beat the eggs with the salt until frothy, using a large fork or whisk. Pour over the onion and spread out evenly. Reduce the heat to low, cover, and cook until the edges of the omelet begin to get firm. Uncover and run a spatula around the edges to keep it from sticking to the pan. When the center of the omelet is almost firm, place a plate over the skillet and invert, dropping the omelet onto the plate. Gently slide it back into the pan. Cover and cook a few minutes until the underside is lightly browned. Slide out onto a plate, roll like a pancake, and cut into strips.

To serve, mound the rice on a heated serving platter. Garnish with the omelet strips. Sprinkle with the melted butter and cinnamon.

• *Variation*
  RICE PILAF WITH EGG (Armenia)
Follow the recipe for Plain Rice Pilaf I (page 144), but before adding the parboiled rice to half of the melted but-

ter in the saucepan, pour in 2 beaten eggs and cook gently over very low heat about 1 minute. Serve the pilaf with pieces of the egg crust which has formed at the bottom of the pan.

Rice Pilaf with Lentils Armenia
[Chalkashovi]

Serves 6

1 cup dried lentils
1½ cups uncooked long-
   grain white rice

8 tablespoons butter

Cook the lentils in lightly salted boiling water about 15 minutes or until nearly tender. Drain thoroughly.

Boil the rice according to the recipe for Plain Rice Pilaf I (page 144). Drain well. Combine it with the lentils and mix well. In a heavy saucepan melt 4 tablespoons of the butter. Add the lentil and rice mixture and sprinkle with the remaining 4 tablespoons butter. Steam the mixture as directed in that recipe.

Note: Caucasian Armenians serve the pilaf with *albukhara* plums which have been slightly sautéed in butter.

Rice Pilaf with Orange Peel and Nuts
Azerbaidzhan

An ancient and superlative pilaf traditionally served at weddings and other important celebrations.

Serves 4

The peel of 2 large, thick-skinned oranges, cut into strips 1 inch long and ⅜ inch wide
½ cup butter
1 cup sugar
¾ cup water
Pinch saffron dissolved in 1 tablespoon warm water

¼ cup unsalted pistachios, shelled and slivered
¼ cup slivered blanched almonds
1 tablespoon freshly squeezed and strained lemon juice
1 recipe Saffron Rice Pilaf with Kazmag (page 147)

In a small saucepan combine the orange peel with lightly salted cold water to cover. Bring to a boil over high heat. Reduce the heat to moderate and cook until soft. Remove from the heat and drain. Rinse thoroughly with cold water. Dry with paper towels and set aside.

In a small saucepan melt the butter over moderate heat. Add the sugar, water, and dissolved saffron and cook, stirring constantly to dissolve the sugar. Add the orange peel, nuts, and lemon juice. Simmer until the peel is sweet, the mixture is thickened, and most of the water is gone. Stir occasionally and add a little more water if necessary.

Mound the rice on a heated serving platter. Top with the orange peel and nut mixture, garnish with wedges of *kazmag* crust, and serve.

• *Variation*
Combine 1 cup water and ½ cup sugar in a small saucepan. Bring to a boil, stirring to dissolve the sugar. Add ½
cup each dried apricots and pitted dried prunes, cut into
strips. Simmer until the fruit is tender and most of the
water is absorbed. Combine with the orange peel and nut
mixture and use as a topping for the pilaf.

Rice Pilaf with Dried Fruits Azerbaidzhan [Shirin Plov]

A magnificently rich and glorious pilaf reminiscent of the
color and splendor of the East.

Serves 4

2 tablespoons butter
½ cup dried apricot halves
½ cup pitted dried prunes
½ cup dried currants
⅓ cup sugar or to taste
1½ cups uncooked long-
grain white rice

1 teaspoon vegetable oil or
Clarified Butter (page
262)
4 tablespoons melted
butter, preferably
Clarified Butter
Melted butter to taste

In a heavy skillet melt the butter over moderate heat. Reduce the heat to low, add the dried fruits, and sauté until
heated through, stirring frequently. Sprinkle with the
sugar and cook a minute or so longer. Remove from the
heat and set aside.

Boil the rice according to the recipe for Rice Pilaf with
Kazmag (page 146). Drain. Prepare the *kazmag* as di-

rected. Brush the bottom of a heavy casserole with the oil and line it with the *kazmag*. Coat the *kazmag* generously with some of the melted butter. Distribute half of the parboiled rice evenly over it. Spread the sautéed fruit mixture over the entire surface, then cover with the rest of the rice. Sprinkle with the remaining melted butter. Place a kitchen towel over the casserole. Put the lid on and bring the corners of the towel over it. Fasten them there to keep them away from the flame. The cloth will absorb the steam as it rises from the rice, leaving the grains dry and separate. Simmer over very low heat 30 to 40 minutes or until the rice is done.

Mound the rice on a heated serving platter. Top with the fruit mixture. Garnish with wedges of *kazmag* crust. Sprinkle with the melted butter and serve.

• *Variations*

A similar pilaf called *Meyva Plov* omits the sugar.

An Armenian version substitutes seedless raisins for the currants, uses only 1 tablespoon sugar, and adds ¼ teaspoon ground cloves or to taste with the sugar. The sautéed fruit mixture is used as a topping for Plain Rice Pilaf (pages 144–145). Sprinkle with cinnamon just before serving.

RICE PILAF WITH DRIED FRUITS AND ALMONDS (Armenia)

Sauté ¼ cup whole blanched almonds in approximately ½ tablespoon butter until golden, stirring frequently. Add 2 tablespoons butter to the skillet and heat. Add ½ cup dried apricots, quartered, ½ cup dates, quartered, and ½ cup seedless golden raisins and turn them in the butter until the fruits are thoroughly heated through. Sprinkle with cinnamon and mix well. Serve as a topping for Plain Rice Pilaf (pages 144–145) or Saffron Rice Pilaf (page 145).

Flaming Holiday Pilaf Armenia
[Donagan Plav]

Distinguished in both appearance and flavor, this dramatic pilaf provides a spectacular yet simple-to-make dish for a festive occasion.

Serves 8

3 tablespoons butter
2 cups seedless golden raisins
1⅓ cups dried apricots
⅔ cup water (approximately)
¼ cup sugar or to taste
2 recipes Plain Rice Pilaf II (page 145)
Baked Quinces (page 204)
Baked Apples (page 204)
Warmed brandy

In a small skillet melt the butter over moderate heat. Add the raisins and sauté until golden brown, stirring frequently. Remove from the heat and keep warm.

In a small saucepan combine the dried apricots with the water and the sugar. Cook gently until the liquid in the pan is absorbed and the apricots are just tender and still intact, not mushy. Add them to the raisins and mix together.

On a large round serving platter mound the hot pilaf in the shape of a mountain. Cover with the dried fruit mixture. Place the baked quinces and apples alternately around the pilaf. With the long handle of a spoon make a hole in the center of the pilaf. Line the opening with aluminum foil and fill it with the warmed brandy. Ignite the brandy, turn off the lights, and serve.

Note: ¾ cup blanched almonds sautéed in butter may be added to the dried fruits.

Rice Pilaf with Fish and Dried Fruits
[Balig Plov]

An interesting and unusual Azerbaidzhani pilaf.

Serves 4

1½ pounds red snapper
6 tablespoons butter
1 large onion, finely
   chopped
½ cup dried apricots,
   washed, drained, and
   chopped
¾ cup dried currants,
   washed and drained

Salt and freshly ground
   black pepper to taste
1 recipe Plain Rice Pilaf I
   (page 144)
¼ teaspoon powdered
   saffron dissolved in 1
   tablespoon warm water
Melted butter to taste

Wash the fish under running cold water and dry
thoroughly with paper towels. Cut into small serving
pieces. In a heavy skillet heat 2 tablespoons of the butter
over moderate heat. Add the onion and sauté until golden
brown, stirring frequently. Remove to a plate and set
aside. Add the remaining 4 tablespoons butter to the skillet and heat. Add the fish and sauté on all sides. Return the
onion to the skillet. Add the apricots, currants, and salt and
pepper. Mix carefully so as not to break the fish. Cover and
simmer gently 10 to 15 minutes, adding a tablespoon or so
of hot water if the mixture seems too dry.

To serve, spoon about 1 cup of the rice into a small
bowl. Add the dissolved saffron and mix gently until the
rice turns yellow. Mound the remaining rice on a heated
serving platter. Garnish with the saffron rice. Top with the
fish and fruit mixture and sprinkle with the melted butter.

Note: In the Caucasus cornelian cherries are substituted for the apricots. A pinch or more of saffron dissolved in 1 tablespoon warm water may be added with the fruits.

Rice Pilaf with Chicken and Dried Fruits
Azerbaidzhan
[Juja Plov]

Oriental opulence is expressed in this most aristocratic of pilafs, meant, understandably, for great occasions.

Serves 4

2 tablespoons butter
½ cup dried apricot halves
1 cup dried currants
1 recipe Plain Rice Pilaf I
 (page 144)
¼ teaspoon powdered

saffron dissolved in 1
 tablespoon warm water
2 recipes Pressed Fried
 Chicken (page 84),
 omitting the garlic
Melted butter to taste

In a small skillet melt the butter over moderate heat. Add the apricots and currants and sauté, stirring frequently. Remove from the heat and set aside.

Spoon about 1 cup of the rice into a small bowl. Add the dissolved saffron and mix gently until the rice turns yellow. Mound the remaining rice on a heated serving platter. Garnish with the saffron rice. Top with the fried chicken and the fruit mixture. Sprinkle with the melted butter.

• *Variation*
Another popular pilaf is prepared with roast chicken that
has been stuffed with a mixture of dried pitted cornelian
cherries, dried currants, and minced onion sautéed in butter. The chicken is served over a mound of Rice Pilaf with
Kazmag (page 146), sprinkled with melted butter, and garnished with wedges of *kazmag* crust.

Rice Pilaf with Chicken Chigirtma
Azerbaidzhan
[Plov Chigirtma]

Serves 4

2 pounds chicken, boned
    and cut into 1½- to 2-
    inch pieces
2 tablespoons butter
1 medium onion, finely
    chopped
Juice of 1 lemon, freshly
    squeezed and strained
Cinnamon to taste
Salt and freshly ground
    black pepper to taste

4 eggs
¼ cup finely chopped
    fresh dill or to taste
1 recipe Plain Rice Pilaf I
    (page 144)
¼ teaspoon powdered
    saffron dissolved in 1
    tablespoon warm water
Melted butter to taste

Dry the chicken pieces thoroughly with paper towels. In a
large heavy skillet with an ovenproof handle melt the butter over moderate heat. Add the chicken and sauté, turning
and regulating the heat as needed until it is browned on
all sides and cooked through. Transfer the chicken to a

plate, leaving the butter in the pan. Add the onion to the skillet and sauté until lightly browned, stirring frequently. Add the lemon juice, cinnamon, and salt and pepper and mix well. Return the chicken to the skillet and baste it thoroughly with the mixture. In a small bowl beat the eggs with a pinch of salt until frothy, then beat in the dill. Pour over the chicken. Bake in a preheated 375° oven about 15 minutes or until the eggs are firm. Remove from the oven. Cut into diamonds and keep warm.

Spoon about 1 cup of the rice into a small bowl. Add the dissolved saffron and mix gently until the rice turns yellow. Mound the remaining rice on a heated serving platter. Garnish with the saffron rice. Top with the Chicken *Chigirtma*. Sprinkle with cinnamon and the melted butter and serve.

Note: A pinch of powdered saffron or more dissolved in 1 tablespoon warm water may be substituted for the lemon juice, in which case the pilaf is served with lemon wedges.

Rice Pilaf with Goose and Prunes
Azerbaidzhan
[Gaz Kavourma Plov]

Serves 4

3 pounds goose, trimmed
of all fat and cut into
1½- to 2-ounce pieces
Salt to taste
4 tablespoons butter,
preferably Clarified
Butter (page 262)
1 medium onion, cut
lengthwise in half and
sliced

¼ pound pitted dried
prunes, washed
½ teaspoon powdered
saffron dissolved in 2
tablespoons warm water
1 recipe Plain Rice Pilaf I
(page 144)
Melted butter to taste

Season the pieces of goose with salt. In a heavy skillet melt the butter over moderate heat. Add the goose pieces and fry gently, turning to brown all over and regulating the heat as necessary until it is tender. Remove to a plate and keep warm. Add the onion to the skillet and sauté until golden brown, stirring frequently. Return the goose to the skillet. Add the prunes and 1 tablespoon of the dissolved saffron. Reduce the heat, cover, and simmer 15 minutes, adding a little hot water if the mixture seems dry.

To serve, spoon about 1 cup of the rice into a small bowl. Add the remaining 1 tablespoon dissolved saffron and mix gently until the rice turns yellow. Mound the rest of the rice on a heated serving platter. Garnish with the saffron rice. Top with the goose mixture and sprinkle with the melted butter.

Rice Pilaf with Lamb and White Beans
Azerbaidzhan
[Plov Lobi-Chilov]

Even the lowly bean becomes a feast for a king in this nourishing and flavorful pilaf.

Serves 4

3 tablespoons butter
1 pound boneless lean lamb, cut into 1-inch cubes
1 medium onion, finely chopped
1½ cups beef broth
Salt and freshly ground black pepper to taste
Pinch or more powdered saffron dissolved in 1 tablespoon warm water (optional)
1 cup uncooked long-grain white rice
¼ teaspoon powdered

saffron dissolved in 1 tablespoon warm water
1 15-ounce can Great Northern beans, drained and rinsed
1 teaspoon vegetable oil or Clarified Butter (page 262)
4 tablespoons melted butter, preferably Clarified Butter
½ cup dried currants or seedless raisins
Melted butter to taste
Cinnamon

In a heavy casserole melt 2 tablespoons of the butter over moderate heat. Add the lamb and onion and sauté until the lamb is browned on all sides, stirring frequently. Add the broth, salt and pepper, and, if desired, the pinch of dissolved saffron. Bring to a boil over high heat. Reduce the heat to low, cover, and simmer about 1 hour or until the lamb is tender. When done, most of the liquid in the casserole should have been absorbed. If not, reduce it by fast boiling, uncovered.

Boil the rice according to the recipe for Rice Pilaf with Kazmag (page 146). Drain. Mix it gently but thoroughly with the dissolved saffron. Combine it with the beans. Prepare the *kazmag* as directed. Brush the bottom of a heavy casserole with the oil and line it with the *kazmag*. Cover the *kazmag* with 2 tablespoons of the melted butter. Add the rice and bean mixture. Sprinkle evenly with the remaining 2 tablespoons melted butter. Place a kitchen towel over the casserole. Put the lid on and bring the corners of the towel over it. Fasten them there to keep them away from the flame. The cloth will absorb the steam as it rises from the rice, leaving the grains dry and separate. Simmer over very low heat about 40 minutes.

In a small skillet melt the remaining 1 tablespoon butter over low heat. Add the currants and sauté until heated through, stirring frequently.

To serve, mound the pilaf on a heated serving platter and place the lamb stew and sautéed currants next to it. Sprinkle it with the melted butter and cinnamon and garnish with wedges of *kazmag* crust.

Note: ¾ cup dried beans may be used instead of the canned ones. Drop them into boiling salted water and boil 1 to 2 minutes. Remove from the heat and let the beans soak, uncovered, 1 hour. Return to boiling, reduce the heat, and simmer, uncovered, about 1 hour or until the beans are tender but not mushy. Drain thoroughly.

Rice Pilaf with Lentils, Lamb, and Currants Azerbaidzhan
[Myarji Plov]

A supremely gratifying pilaf with a rustic quality and much character.

Serves 4

3 tablespoons butter
1 pound boneless lean
  lamb, cut into 1-inch
  cubes
1 medium onion, finely
  chopped
1½ cups beef broth
Salt and freshly ground
  black pepper to taste

½ cup dried currants or
  seedless raisins
1 recipe Rice Pilaf with
  Lentils (page 151)
¼ teaspoon powdered
  saffron dissolved in
  1 tablespoon warm
  water (optional)
Cinnamon

In a heavy casserole melt 2 tablespoons of the butter over moderate heat. Add the lamb and onion and sauté until the lamb is browned on all sides, stirring frequently. Add the broth and salt and pepper. Bring to a boil over high heat. Reduce the heat to low, cover, and simmer 45 minutes.

Meanwhile, in a small skillet heat the remaining 1 tablespoon butter over moderate heat. Add the currants, reduce the heat to low, and turn the currants in the butter until heated through. Add to the lamb, stir gently, and simmer, covered, 15 minutes or until the lamb is tender. When done, most of the liquid in the pan should have been absorbed. If not, reduce it by fast boiling, uncovered.

Prepare the Rice Pilaf with Lentils. If desired, before combining the parboiled rice with the lentils, you may mix it with the dissolved saffron.

To serve, mound the pilaf on a heated serving platter. Top with the lamb stew and sprinkle with the cinnamon.

Note: Instead of the lamb, this pilaf is sometimes served with an omelet flavored with minced fried onion and lemon juice (see Rice Pilaf with Omelet, page 150).

Rice Pilaf with Lamb Chigirtma
Azerbaidzhan
[Plov Chigirtma]

Serves 4

3 tablespoons butter
1 pound boneless lean lamb, cut into ¾-inch cubes
1 large onion, finely chopped
1 cup beef broth
2 tablespoons freshly squeezed and strained lemon juice
Pinch or more powdered saffron dissolved in 1 tablespoon warm water

Salt and freshly ground black pepper to taste
4 eggs
1 recipe Plain Rice Pilaf I (page 144)
¼ teaspoon powdered saffron dissolved in 1 tablespoon warm water
Melted butter to taste
Cinnamon

In a heavy skillet with an ovenproof handle melt the butter over moderate heat. Add the lamb and onion and sauté until the lamb is browned on all sides, stirring frequently.

Add the broth, lemon juice, pinch dissolved saffron, and the salt and pepper. Cover and simmer about 40 minutes or until the meat is tender. If the liquid in the skillet is not absorbed by the time the lamb is done, reduce it by fast boiling, uncovered. If it is absorbed before the lamb is tender, add a little more broth and cook further.

Beat the eggs well with a pinch of salt. Pour over the meat and mix well. Bake in a preheated 450° oven about 5 to 7 minutes or until the eggs are firm.

To serve, spoon about 1 cup of the rice into a small bowl. Add the ¼ teaspoon dissolved saffron and mix gently until the rice turns yellow. Mound the remaining rice on a heated serving platter. Garnish with the saffron rice and top with the Lamb *Chigirtma*. Sprinkle with the melted butter and cinnamon.

• *Variation*
RICE PILAF WITH GROUND LAMB CHIGIRTMA
(Giymya Chigirtma Plov)
Sauté 1 pound lean ground lamb and 1 large minced onion in 3 tablespoons butter, stirring frequently. Season with salt and pepper and cinnamon to taste. Beat 4 eggs with a pinch of salt. Pour over the lamb and mix well. Bake as above. Prepare 1 recipe Saffron Rice Pilaf (page 145). Mound it on a heated serving platter and top with the ground Lamb *Chigirtma*. Sprinkle with the melted butter and serve.

Rice Pilaf with Lamb, Dried Fruits, and Chestnuts
[Plov Parcha Doshyamya]

A superb combination highly esteemed by Azerbaidzhanis, who have created a series of fascinating pilafs on
this exquisite theme.

Serves 4

2 tablespoons butter
1 pound boneless lean
    lamb, cut into 1-inch
    cubes
1 medium onion, finely
    chopped
2½ cups beef broth
Salt and freshly ground
    black pepper to taste

⅔ cup dried currants
½ cup dried apricots
¼ pound chestnuts,
    shelled and peeled
    (page 167)
1 recipe Rice Pilaf with
    Kazmag (page 146)
Melted butter to taste
Cinnamon

In a heavy skillet melt the butter over moderate heat. Add
the lamb and onion and sauté until the lamb is browned
on all sides, stirring frequently. Add the broth and salt and
pepper. Bring to a boil over high heat. Reduce the heat to
low, cover, and simmer 30 minutes. Add the dried fruits
and chestnuts, cover, and simmer 30 minutes or until the
lamb is tender, adding more broth only if necessary. When
done, most of the liquid in the pan should have been absorbed. If not, reduce it by fast boiling, uncovered.

    To serve, mound the rice on a heated serving platter.
Top with the lamb mixture and garnish with wedges of
kazmag crust. Sprinkle with the melted butter and cinnamon.

Note: ¼ to ½ teaspoon ground cumin or curry powder may be added with the dried fruits.

Azerbaidzhanis living in the Caucasus vary this dish by substituting persimmons for the apricots.

Rice Pilaf with Lamb, Pumpkin, Dried Fruits, and Chestnuts Azerbaidzhan [Plov Kham Doshyamya]

Serves 4

¼ pound chestnuts
4 tablespoons butter
½ cup dried apricots
½ cup dried prunes
½ cup dried currants
½ pound pumpkin, peeled and cut into ½-inch-thick by 1½-inch-long slices
1 pound boneless lean lamb, cut into ½-inch cubes

Salt and freshly ground black pepper to taste
1½ cups uncooked long-grain white rice
4 tablespoons melted butter, preferably Clarified Butter (page 262)
Melted butter to taste

Slit the chestnuts halfway around with a sharp knife. Place them in a saucepan. Cover with cold water and bring to a boil. Boil 5 minutes. Remove from the heat. With a slotted spoon lift out the chestnuts, a few at a time, and shell and skin them quickly while they are still hot. Set aside any that cannot be peeled and drop them all later into boiling water for 1 minute, then peel them one at a time.

In a small skillet melt 2 tablespoons of the butter over moderate heat. Add the apricots and prunes, lower the heat, and turn them in the butter until they are heated through. Add the currants and continue to stir until the fruits are golden brown. Remove to a plate and keep warm. Place 1 tablespoon butter in the skillet and heat. Add the peeled chestnuts and sauté until lightly browned, stirring frequently. Add to the fruits and keep warm. Place the remaining 1 tablespoon butter in the skillet and heat. Add the pumpkin slices and sauté until golden brown on both sides, using more butter if necessary. Remove from the heat and combine with the fruits and chestnuts.

Season the lamb with the salt and pepper. Boil the rice according to the recipe for Plain Rice Pilaf I (page 144). Place 2 tablespoons of the melted butter in a heavy casserole and heat. Distribute half of the parboiled rice evenly over it. Spread the lamb and sautéed fruit mixture over the entire surface, then cover with the rest of the rice. Sprinkle with the remaining 2 tablespoons melted butter. Place a kitchen towel over the casserole. Put the lid on and bring the corners of the towel over it. Fasten them there to keep them away from the flame. The cloth will absorb the steam as it rises from the rice, leaving the grains dry and separate. Simmer over very low heat 30 to 40 minutes or until the lamb is tender.

To serve, mound the rice on a heated serving platter. Put the lamb next to it and surround with the fruit mixture. Sprinkle with the melted butter.

• *Variations*
You may omit steaming the fruit mixture with the rice and meat. Simply sauté them and serve with the steamed rice and lamb as above. If you like, you may sprinkle the fruit mixture with a little sugar and cinnamon.

This dish may also be prepared with meat patties rather than cubed lamb. Grind the meat twice, season with salt, pepper, ½ teaspoon cinnamon, and, if desired, 1 medium grated onion. Knead until the mixture is well blended and smooth. Form into small, hamburger-shaped patties. Place them between the 2 layers of the parboiled rice and proceed as above.

Note: In the Caucasus dried *albukhara* plums and persimmons are used along with the apricots and currants in the preparation of this pilaf.

Rice Pilaf with Ground Lamb, Dried Fruit, and Chestnut Topping
[Giymya Plov]

This colorful and decorative Azerbaidzhani pilaf provides a sumptuous feast as exciting to the eye as to the palate.

Serves 4

5 tablespoons butter
1 pound lean ground lamb
1 medium onion, finely
 chopped
⅔ cup dried currants
⅔ cup dried pitted prunes
2 ounces chestnuts,

shelled, peeled, and
 chopped (page 167)
1 recipe Saffron Rice Pilaf
 with Kazmag (page 146)
Melted butter to taste
Cinnamon

In a heavy skillet heat 3 tablespoons of the butter over moderate heat. Add the lamb and onion and sauté until the meat turns brown, stirring and breaking it up with a fork. Remove from the heat and keep warm.

In a small skillet melt the remaining 2 tablespoons butter over moderate heat. Add the currants and prunes, reduce the heat to low, and sauté until heated through, stirring frequently. Add the chestnuts and continue to sauté until the fruits are golden brown. Remove from the heat, add to the lamb, and mix well.

To serve, mound the rice on a heated serving platter. Top with the lamb mixture and garnish with wedges of *kazmag* crust. Sprinkle with the melted butter and cinnamon.

Note: In the Caucasus dried pitted cornelian cherries are substituted for the prunes.

Plain Bulghur Pilaf

Serves 4

3 tablespoons butter or
  olive oil
1 small onion, finely
  chopped

1 cup coarse bulghur
1¾ cups chicken or beef
  broth
Salt to taste

In a heavy saucepan heat the butter over moderate heat. Add the onion and sauté until soft and golden, stirring frequently. Add the bulghur and sauté until lightly browned, stirring constantly. Pour in the broth and season with the salt. Mix well and bring to a boil. Reduce the heat to low, cover, and simmer about 20 minutes or until all the liquid is absorbed and the bulghur is tender but still somewhat firm, not mushy. If necessary, a little more broth may be added. Serve as an accompaniment to stews, poultry, and meat dishes.

Note: ½ teaspoon ground coriander, ¼ teaspoon ground cumin, and, if desired, ¼ teaspoon ground cardamom may be stirred into the bulghur before adding the broth.

Bulghur Pilaf with Vermicelli and Cheese
Armenia

Serves 4
Follow the recipe for Plain Bulghur Pilaf (above), sautéing 1 clove garlic, finely chopped, and ½ cup vermicelli, broken into 1-inch pieces, in the butter or olive oil along with the onion. Add the bulghur and proceed as directed. When done, stir in ½ cup grated Parmesan or Gruyère cheese and 1 tablespoon finely chopped parsley. This may be served mixed with or accompanied by fried eggplant slices.

Bulghur Pilaf with Mussels Armenia
[Midia Plav]

Serves 8

40 mussels in the shell
⅔ cup olive oil
4 medium onions, finely
   chopped
1 cup coarse bulghur
2 tablespoons pine nuts
2 medium tomatoes,
   peeled, seeded, and
   finely chopped

¼ cup dried currants
1½ cups beef broth or
   water
Salt and freshly ground
   black pepper to taste
Lemon wedges
Parsley or dill sprigs

Scrub the mussels thoroughly and place in cold water to cover. Pry open 30 of the mussels with the point of a sharp knife. Trim off the beards, scoop out the flesh, and discard the shells. Set aside, along with the remaining 10 unopened mussels.

In a heavy skillet heat the oil over moderate heat. Add the onions and sauté until soft but not browned, stirring frequently. Add the bulghur and nuts and sauté 5 minutes, stirring constantly. Add the tomatoes and sauté 5 minutes, stirring. Add the currants, broth, salt and pepper, and the opened mussels. Mix carefully. Scatter the unopened mussels on top, inserting them into the bulghur mixture without stirring. Cover and cook 5 minutes over high heat. Reduce the heat to low and simmer 15 to 20 minutes or until all the liquid is absorbed and the bulghur is tender. Remove from the heat. Take off the lid, stretch a kitchen towel over the top of the pan, and replace the lid. Leave in a warm place 20 minutes.

Mound the pilaf on a heated serving dish. Surround with the mussels in shells and garnish with the lemon wedges and parsley. Serve cold as an appetizer.

Note: ¼ cup minced fresh dill or to taste may be added with the broth or stirred into the pilaf just before removing it from the heat. Some people also add 1 to 2 teaspoons sugar with the broth. Two cans (5 ounces each) mussels may be substituted for the fresh ones. Place the drained mussels in a sieve and rinse thoroughly under running cold water. Remove any black spots.

Bulghur Pilaf with Dried Fruit and Nut Topping Armenia

A delightfully unusual way of preparing this nutritious, nut-flavored cereal.

Serves 4

2 tablespoons butter
⅓ cup whole blanched
  almonds
¾ cup dried apricot halves
¾ cup golden seedless
  raisins

1 recipe Plain Bulghur
  Pilaf (page 170)
  prepared with butter

In a heavy skillet melt the butter over moderate heat. Reduce the heat to low, add the almonds, apricots, and raisins, and sauté until the nuts turn golden, stirring frequently. Remove from the heat. Mound the pilaf on a heated serving platter. Top with the fruit mixture and serve with poultry or meat.

Note: You may sprinkle ¼ teaspoon cinnamon over the sautéed fruit mixture.

10. SAVORY PASTRIES AND PASTAS

Savory pastries are an integral part of Caucasian cooking. They are made in various traditional shapes and sizes: half-moons, triangles, squares, diamond-shaped tarts, and open-faced as well as closed pies. They can be prepared with different doughs ranging from simple bread and pie dough to flaky pastry and are filled with cheese, ground meat, or vegetables. Small-size pastries make excellent appetizers, while larger ones can provide a light main course when accompanied by a salad or soup.

I have also included in this chapter a number of recipes prepared with homemade as well as commercially packaged pasta. At what stage of Caucasian cooking these dishes originated I do not know, but they have certainly been evolving for many centuries and continue to enjoy a widespread popularity in the Caucasus. *Arishta*, for instance, though similar to Italian pasta, is actually of Oriental origin and has been known in Transcaucasia since ancient times. Often flavored with ingredients such as cinnamon, coriander, dill, yogurt, pomegranate juice, and *sumakh,* Caucasian pasta specialties provide delicious as well as nutritious and economical recipes quite different from ordinary pasta dishes.

Homemade Egg Noodles
[Arishta]

Serves 4

2 cups sifted all-purpose flour

2 eggs

3 to 4 tablespoons cold water

½ teaspoon salt

Put the flour into a large mixing bowl. Make a hollow in the middle and add the eggs, 3 tablespoons of the water, and the salt. Gradually mix the flour into the liquid ingredients until the dough can be formed into a rough ball, adding more water only if necessary.

Knead the dough on a floured surface about 10 minutes or until smooth and elastic, working in a little more flour if it seems sticky. Cover with a kitchen towel and let rest about 20 minutes.

Divide the dough into 2 equal parts. Roll out 1 part on a floured board or pastry cloth until paper-thin, sprinkling both the surface of the dough and under it with flour as needed to prevent sticking. Leave the dough on a cloth to rest and dry about 15 minutes. Roll up like a jelly roll and with a sharp knife cut into ¼-inch strips. Unroll the strips and set them aside on waxed paper. Repeat with the second half of dough.

Use the freshly made noodles according to directions given in recipes calling for them elsewhere in this book. Or, cook them in plenty of lightly salted boiling water about 5 to 7 minutes or until just tender, stirring often to prevent them from sticking to the bottom of the pan. Drain quickly but thoroughly. They may be served with melted butter or sour cream.

Noodle, Spinach, and Cheese Casserole
Armenia

This makes an excellent luncheon or supper entrée, as well as a pleasant accompaniment to meat and poultry.

Serves 6

¼ cup olive oil or butter
1 medium onion, finely chopped
1 pound spinach, washed, stemmed, and chopped
2 tablespoons finely chopped fresh dill or 1 tablespoon dried dill weed (optional)
Salt and freshly ground black pepper to taste

8 ounces medium wide egg noodles
4 tablespoons butter
4 tablespoons flour
2 cups milk
½ pound Gruyère, Parmesan, or Romano cheese, shredded
White pepper

In a heavy skillet heat the oil over moderate heat. Add the onion and sauté until soft but not browned, stirring frequently. Add the spinach and dill and simmer 10 to 15 minutes or until tender, stirring frequently. Season with the salt and pepper. Remove from the heat and reserve.

Cook the noodles according to package directions. Drain well in a colander. Return to the pan and toss gently but thoroughly with 2 tablespoons of the butter. Set aside.

In a small saucepan melt the remaining 2 tablespoons butter over low heat. Add the flour and cook about 3 minutes, stirring constantly. Gradually add the milk, stirring continuously with a wire whisk. Simmer until the sauce is smooth, thick, and hot. Add ¾ of the cheese and stir until it is melted. Season to taste with additional salt and the white pepper. Remove from the heat.

In a buttered casserole arrange alternate layers of noodles, spinach, and cream sauce, beginning and ending with noodles. Sprinkle evenly with the remaining cheese. Bake in a preheated 350° oven about 45 minutes or until the top turns golden brown.

Pasta with Ground Lamb Azerbaidzhan [Giymya Khingal]

Serves 4

5 tablespoons butter
1 pound lean ground lamb
1 medium onion, finely
chopped
Salt and freshly ground
black pepper to taste
1 tablespoon freshly
squeezed and strained
lemon juice

1 recipe Egg Noodle
Dough (page 175)
Cinnamon
Freshly grated Parmesan
cheese
Garlic Yogurt Sauce (page
214)

In a heavy skillet melt 3 tablespoons of the butter over moderate heat. Add the lamb and onion and sauté until the meat turns brown, stirring and breaking it up with a fork. Sprinkle with the salt and pepper and lemon juice and mix well. Remove from the heat and keep warm.

On a lightly floured surface roll out 1 ball of dough into a rough rectangle almost as thin as paper, sprinkling both the surface of the dough and under it with flour as needed to prevent sticking. Cut into small diamonds. Repeat with the second ball of dough.

Cook the diamonds of dough in plenty of lightly salted boiling water about 5 to 7 minutes or until just tender, stirring often to prevent them from sticking to the bottom of the pan. Drain quickly but thoroughly in a colander and return to the pan. Add the remaining 2 tablespoons butter, mix well, and turn into a heated serving dish. Top with the lamb mixture. Sprinkle with the cinnamon and ½ cup of the grated cheese. Serve at once, accompanied by a bowl of Garlic Yogurt Sauce and additional grated cheese on the side.

Note: In the Caucasus, *brindza* cheese (page 259) is used for this dish. If you are in a hurry, you may substitute packaged pasta such as wide egg noodles for the homemade pasta. Cook according to package directions, drain, and proceed as above.

Stuffed Meat Dumplings Azerbaidzhan
[Kyurza]

Serves 4

4 tablespoons butter
½ pound lean ground
   lamb
1 medium onion, finely
   chopped
Salt and freshly ground
   black pepper to taste

1 recipe Egg Noodle
   Dough (page 175)
Cinnamon
Unflavored yogurt

In a heavy skillet melt 2 tablespoons of the butter over moderate heat. Add the lamb and onion and sauté until the meat turns brown, stirring frequently and breaking it up with a fork. Season with the salt and pepper. Remove from the heat and set aside.

On a lightly floured surface roll out 1 ball of dough very thin, almost as thin as paper, sprinkling both the surface of the dough and under it with flour as needed to prevent sticking. Cut out as many circles of dough as you can with a 3-inch cookie cutter. Place about 1½ teaspoons of the meat mixture in the lower half of each circle. Dip a finger in cold water and moisten the edges. Fold over the other half to make a half-moon. Seal the edges by pressing firmly with the prongs of a fork.

Drop the dumplings, a dozen at a time, into lightly salted boiling water. Simmer, uncovered, 7 to 10 minutes or until they rise to the surface. With a slotted spoon transfer them to paper towels to drain. Place in a heated serving dish. Top with any remaining meat mixture. Sprinkle with the cinnamon and serve accompanied by a bowl of the yogurt on the side.

Note: For larger dumplings, cut the dough into circles of 4 to 5 inches in diameter and use 2 to 3 teaspoons meat mixture for each circle. A Georgian version uses a combination of lamb and pork rather than lamb alone, while an Armenian one substitutes beef.

Azerbaidzhani Lamb Pastries
[Kutab]

Serves 12

½ pound lean lamb, ground twice
1 small onion, finely chopped
1 tablespoon freshly squeezed pomegranate juice or lemon juice
½ teaspoon cinnamon
Salt and freshly ground black pepper to taste

1 recipe Egg Noodle Dough (page 175)
4 tablespoons Clarified Butter (page 262) or 2 tablespoons butter and 2 tablespoons vegetable oil
Sumakh (page 266)
Unflavored yogurt (optional)

In a large mixing bowl combine the lamb, onion, pomegranate juice, cinnamon, and salt and pepper. Knead until well blended and smooth. Taste for seasoning.

Roll out the dough into circles, stuff with the meat mixture, and shape into half-moons as described in the recipe for Stuffed Meat Dumplings (page 179).

In a heavy skillet heat the Clarified Butter over high heat. Add the pastries, a batch at a time, and reduce the heat to moderate. Fry until the pastries are golden brown on both sides and cooked through, adding more Clarified Butter to the pan if necessary. Transfer them to an oven-proof platter and keep warm in a preheated 250° oven while you fry the remaining pastries. Serve at once, sprinkled with the *sumakh* and accompanied by the yogurt.

• *Variation*
HERB PASTRIES
Sauté 2 bunches scallions, minced, including 2 inches of the green tops, in 2 tablespoons Clarified Butter until soft but not browned. Add 1 pound fresh spinach, stemmed and minced (or use ½ pound each spinach and sorrel), ¼ cup minced fresh coriander leaves or parsley, and ¼ cup minced fresh dill. Cover and simmer until the greens are tender. Remove from the heat. Season to taste with fresh pomegranate juice or lemon juice, cinnamon, and salt and pepper. Mix well. Stuff the dough rounds with this mixture and fry as above. Serve topped with melted butter and accompanied by unflavored yogurt.

You may plunge the spinach and herbs into boiling water for a minute or two and drain before sautéing them in the butter. Also, you may omit sautéing the coriander and dill. Simply add them with the seasonings.

Note: In the Caucasus, pomegranate seeds, Pomegranate Syrup (page 219), or pomegranate paste is often substituted for the pomegranate juice.

Another popular Azerbaidzhani filling for these pastries consists of steamed and pureed pumpkin flavored with minced fried onion, fresh pomegranate juice, cinnamon, and salt and pepper.

Armenian Cheese Pastries
[Banirov Boereg]

This great favorite seems to appeal to every palate and makes a splendid appetizer or first course. Trays of delectable golden *boeregs* invariably make their appearance at parties and celebrations only to vanish almost instantaneously!

Serves 12

PASTRY

2 cups all-purpose flour
½ teaspoon cream of tartar
¾ teaspoon salt

½ pound butter
6 tablespoons water
  (approximately)

CHEESE FILLING

2 small eggs
6 ounces mild Muenster
  cheese, grated
6 ounces sharp cheddar
  cheese, grated
¼ cup finely chopped
  parsley

1 tablespoon finely
  chopped fresh dill or
  mint (optional)
Salt to taste
1 egg, lightly beaten (for
  brushing pastries)

Sift the flour, cream of tartar, and salt into a chilled mixing bowl. Cut the butter in finely with a pastry blender or 2 knives. Add enough water to make a soft but not sticky dough. Wrap the dough in waxed paper and refrigerate 30 minutes.

On a lightly floured surface roll the dough into a rectangle about ⅛ inch thick. Beginning with one of the short ends of the dough, fold it into thirds to form a three-layered rectangle. Again, beginning from the short end, fold the dough into thirds to form a square. Cut the dough in half. Wrap the halves separately in waxed paper. Refrigerate 1 hour.

Meanwhile, prepare the filling. Place the eggs in a mixing bowl and beat slightly with a fork. Add the cheeses, parsley, dill, and salt and beat until the mixture is smooth. Set aside.

On a lightly floured board roll out one-half of the pastry at a time to a rectangle about ⅛ inch thick or less. Using a sharp knife, cut the dough into 2-by-3-inch rectangles. Place about 1½ teaspoons of the cheese filling in the lower half of each rectangle. Dip a finger in cold water and moisten the edges. Fold over the other half. Seal the edges with the tines of a fork. Arrange the pastries side by side on an ungreased baking sheet. Repeat the above procedure with the other half of the dough.

Brush the pastries with the beaten egg. Bake in a preheated 400° oven about 15 minutes or until golden brown and baked through. Serve warm as an appetizer.

Note: A combination of 6 ounces small-curd cottage cheese, drained, or Muenster cheese, grated, and 6 ounces feta cheese, grated, can be substituted for the above cheeses.

Georgian Cheese Bread
[Khachapuri]

One of the ultimate treats of the Georgian table, this elegant and versatile cheese bread is made in different shapes and sizes. Serve it as an appetizer, at breakfast or brunch, or at teatime.

Serves 12

DOUGH

½ cup lukewarm milk
  (110° to 115°)
1 package active dry yeast
Sugar

1½ cups all-purpose flour
1 teaspoon salt
4 tablespoons butter,
  softened

CHEESE FILLING

1 pound mild Muenster
  cheese, grated
1 tablespoon butter,
  softened

1 very small egg
1 egg, lightly beaten (for
  brushing pastries)

Pour ¼ cup of the lukewarm milk into a small bowl and sprinkle with the yeast and ¼ teaspoon sugar. Let the mixture stand 2 to 3 minutes, then stir to dissolve the yeast. Place the flour in a large bowl. Make a well in the center and add the remaining ¼ cup milk, the yeast mixture, 1½ teaspoons sugar, the salt, and the butter. With a large spoon stir the center ingredients together, then gradually blend into the flour. Beat until the ingredients are well blended and form a dough. Knead the dough vigorously on a lightly floured surface 10 minutes until it is smooth and elastic, sprinkling with a little flour if necessary to keep it from sticking. Form into a ball and place in a lightly oiled bowl. Dust the dough lightly with flour. Cover loosely with a kitchen towel. Leave to rise in a warm place (85°) free from drafts (such as an unlit oven with a pan of hot water on the bottom rack) about 45 minutes or until doubled in size.

Punch down the dough and leave to rise a second time another 30 minutes or until it again doubles in size.

Meanwhile, prepare the cheese filling. In a large bowl combine the cheese, butter, and egg. Beat vigorously with a spoon until the mixture is well blended and smooth.

Punch down the dough and roll out on a lightly floured

surface to about $^1/_{16}$-inch thickness. Cut it into circles 6 inches in diameter. On each round of dough spread an even layer of 1½ tablespoons cheese filling in an inner circle about 3 inches in diameter, leaving a 1½-inch border uncovered. Draw the edges of the dough up over the filling into the center, covering it and forming 6 even pleats, making a hexagon-shaped pastry. Pinch together the edges of the dough that meet in the center. Arrange the pastries side by side on a buttered baking sheet. Brush with the beaten egg. Allow the pastries to rest 10 minutes, then bake in a preheated 375° oven about 25 minutes or until golden brown. Serve warm.

11. VEGETABLES

In spite of their year-round abundance, vegetables have never held a prime position in the hierarchy of American food. Caucasians, on the other hand, regard them highly and have applied to their preparation much ingenuity and inventiveness. The profusion of vegetables grown in the Caucasus provides ample incentive. Here one finds a great variety in cooking methods and combinations of flavors. The same vegetable can be prepared in many artful ways, with even the most ordinary being transformed into a festive delicacy.

Seldom are vegetables merely boiled, drained, and served. Caucasians team them with fruits; flavor them with walnut, plum, or pomegranate sauce; spice them with cinnamon; season them with onion, garlic, tomato, or herbs; glaze them with melted butter and sugar; top them with minced fresh herbs, scallions, fried onion, grated cheese, or beaten eggs; or serve them with melted butter, sour cream, or yogurt. Vegetables are frequently stuffed; fried, singly or in combination; stewed with tomatoes, onions, spices, and herbs; baked with cheese; and roasted or grilled after being brushed with melted butter or oil.

Armenia is especially noted for the excellence of its vegetables. An enormous variety ripen under the bright sun of the Ararat valley, such as large and succulent tomatoes, firm-textured and almost seedless cucumbers, red or green peppers both sweet and hot, and eggplants with very few seeds and a light pulp devoid of any bitterness. Important vegetable-producing areas also exist in Azerbaidzhan, notably the Lenkoran region in the southeast, and in Georgia. Other common vegetables of the Caucasus include squash, pumpkin, onion, leeks, garlic, okra, beets, potatoes, carrots, cauliflower, asparagus, corn, mushrooms, and various beans and leafy vegetables. In addition quinces, apples, and other fruits are occasionally served in place of vegetables.

Green Beans in Sour Cream and Tomato Sauce

This recipe provides a novel and flavorful way of serving green beans.

Serves 6

1 pound green beans, trimmed and halved crosswise
4 tablespoons butter
1 large onion, cut

2 large tomatoes, peeled, seeded, and chopped
2 tablespoons finely chopped fresh basil
¾ cup sour cream

lengthwise in half and
thinly sliced
1 medium green pepper,
seeded, deribbed, and
chopped

Salt and freshly ground
black pepper to taste

Drop the beans into lightly salted boiling water. Boil, uncovered, about 10 minutes or until tender but still somewhat firm to the bite, not mushy. Drain and set aside.

In a heavy skillet melt the butter over moderate heat.
Add the onion and green pepper and cook until soft but
not browned, stirring frequently. Add the tomatoes and
basil and cook 2 minutes, stirring often. Add the beans,
mix well, and simmer 2 minutes. Beat the sour cream with
the salt and pepper. Stir into the vegetables gently but
thoroughly. Taste for seasoning. Transfer to a serving bowl
and serve immediately.

Green Beans with Garlic Yogurt Sauce

Serves 4

1 pound green beans,
trimmed and halved
crosswise
3 tablespoons butter
1 medium onion, finely
chopped

2 tablespoons finely
chopped parsley
Garlic Yogurt Sauce (page
214)

Drop the beans into lightly salted boiling water. Boil, uncovered, about 10 minutes or until tender but still firm to
the bite, not mushy. Drain and set aside.

In a heavy skillet melt the butter over moderate heat. Add the onion and sauté until golden brown, stirring frequently. Add the beans, mix well, cover, and simmer 5 minutes. Serve sprinkled with the parsley and accompanied by a bowl of Garlic Yogurt Sauce.

• *Variation*
GREEN BEAN OMELET
After simmering the beans and onion 5 minutes, pour 2 beaten eggs over them. Mix well, cover, and cook until the eggs set. Serve sprinkled with fresh parsley or dill and accompanied by Garlic Yogurt Sauce. Or instead of sprinkling the omelet with the herbs, add ¼ cup minced fresh parsley, dill, or tarragon (or a mixture of parsley, coriander, and basil) with the beans. Green bean omelet is often served as a side dish to fried chicken.

Red Beans in Plum Sauce Georgia

The unexpected and brilliant addition of plum sauce converts the humble bean into an exotic delicacy.

Serves 4

1 very small clove garlic
¼ teaspoon salt
Dash cayenne or to taste
¼ teaspoon finely
    chopped fresh basil
3 teaspoons finely
    chopped fresh coriander
    leaves or parsley

¾ teaspoon red wine
    vinegar
1 cup dried red kidney
    beans, cooked, drained,
    and cooled (page 21), or
    2 cups canned red
    kidney beans, drained
    and rinsed under

3½ tablespoons damson   running cold water
  plum jam

Crush the garlic with the salt. Add the cayenne, basil, and
1 teaspoon coriander and mash the mixture to a smooth
paste. Combine the jam and vinegar in a small enameled
or stainless steel pan and boil over high heat, stirring constantly until the jam dissolves. Rub the mixture through a
fine sieve, then gradually beat it into the garlic-and-herb
paste. Add the beans and toss gently but thoroughly until
the beans are coated with the plum sauce. Taste for seasoning. Cover and refrigerate several hours or overnight.
Serve sprinkled with the remaining 2 teaspoons coriander.

Beets with Garlic Yogurt Sauce Armenia
[Borani]

Serves 4

1 pound beets
2 tablespoons butter
1 medium onion, finely
  chopped

Garlic Yogurt Sauce (page
  214)

Remove the tops from the beets, leaving 1 inch of stem.
Wash the beets. Cover with lightly salted boiling water.
Cover and cook ½ hour to 1 hour (longer for old beets) or
until tender. Drain. Dip in cold water and rub off the
skins. Dice the beets. Place in a serving dish and keep
warm.

Meanwhile, in a small skillet melt the butter over moderate heat. Add the onion and sauté until golden brown, stirring frequently. Add to the beets and mix gently but thoroughly. Serve with the Garlic Yogurt Sauce.

Fried Eggplant with Walnut Sauce

Through the centuries Caucasians have evolved some remarkable specialties featuring eggplant. The Armenians share with the Georgians an unbounded admiration for this classic dish.

Serves 4

1 large eggplant
Salt
½ cup vegetable oil or
  olive oil

Walnut Sauce II (page 216)

Remove the stem and hull from the eggplant. Peel lengthwise in ½-inch strips, leaving ½-inch strips of skin in between, making a striped design. Cut crosswise into ⅜-inch-thick slices and lay on paper towels. Sprinkle generously with the salt, weigh down with a heavy object, and let stand 30 minutes. Rinse and dry thoroughly with fresh paper towels.

In a large, heavy skillet heat the oil over high heat. Reduce the heat to moderate, add the eggplant slices, and fry until lightly and evenly browned on both sides. Drain on paper towels and arrange on a serving platter. Serve cold with the Walnut Sauce.

Note: The fried eggplant is also excellent served with Pomegranate Syrup (page 219) or Garlic Yogurt Sauce (page 214).

Eggplant with Green Peppers and Tomatoes Armenia

This winning combination makes an outstanding appetizer.

Serves 6

2 medium eggplants
Salt
½ cup olive oil or as
  needed
2 medium green peppers,
  seeded, deribbed, and
  sliced
1 large onion, cut

lengthwise in half and
  sliced
3 medium tomatoes,
  peeled, seeded, and
  thinly sliced
Freshly ground black
  pepper to taste

Remove the stems and hulls from the eggplants. Peel lengthwise in 1-inch strips, leaving 1-inch strips of skin in between, making a striped design. Cut crosswise in ⅓-inch-thick slices and lay on paper towels. Sprinkle generously with the salt, weigh down with a heavy object, and let stand 30 minutes. Rinse and dry thoroughly with fresh paper towels.

In a large, heavy skillet heat the oil over high heat. Reduce the heat to moderate, add the eggplant slices, and fry until golden brown on both sides. Remove to a plate and set aside. Fry the green peppers in the oil remaining in the skillet until golden brown on both sides, adding more oil if necessary. Transfer to a plate. Add the onion to the skillet and fry until golden brown, using more oil if necessary. Return the eggplants and green peppers to the skillet. Add the tomatoes and season to taste with salt and pepper. Cover and cook over low heat about ½ hour or until the vegetables are tender and most of the juices in the pan have evaporated.

Serve cold, accompanied by crusty bread and, if you like, a bowl of unflavored yogurt or Garlic Yogurt Sauce (page 214).

Grilled Mushrooms

Serves 4

2 pounds large even-size
  mushrooms
2 tablespoons melted
  butter
Salt to taste
4 scallions, finely

chopped, including 2
  inches of the green tops
2 tablespoons finely
  chopped parsley
Lemon wedges

Wash the mushrooms. Remove and discard the stems. Drop the mushroom tops into boiling water 1 minute. Drain, rinse in cold water, and dry with paper towels. Thread the mushrooms on skewers. Brush with the melted butter. Sprinkle with the salt. Grill slowly, preferably over charcoal, until evenly browned on all sides, turning frequently. Slide the mushrooms off the skewers onto a heated serving platter. Sprinkle with the scallions and parsley and serve with the lemon wedges.

Potatoes in Sour Cream

Serves 4

16 new potatoes
Boiling water to cover
1 cup sour cream
Salt to taste
4 scallions, finely

chopped, including 2
inches of the green tops
⅓ cup finely chopped
fresh dill

Drop the potatoes into the boiling water, cover, and cook about 20 minutes or until tender. Drain and peel while hot. Combine with the sour cream and salt and toss gently. Sprinkle with the scallions and dill and serve.

● *Variation*
Instead of the sour cream, toss the potatoes with melted butter, then sprinkle with salt, scallions, and dill and serve.

Fried Pumpkin Armenia

Inventive Caucasian cooks have learned to prepare pumpkin in many fascinating ways. The following recipe makes an excellent companion to roast turkey or pork.

Serves 4

2 pounds pumpkin
8 tablespoons butter,
  preferably Clarified
  Butter (page 262)

Salt and sugar to taste
1 large onion, finely
  chopped

Remove the seeds and fibers from the pumpkin. Peel and cut the pumpkin into about 1½-inch-long and ¼- to ½-inch-thick slices. In a heavy skillet, melt 6 tablespoons of the butter over moderate heat. Add the pumpkin slices and fry until golden brown on both sides. Sprinkle with the salt and sugar and mix gently, being careful not to mash or break the pumpkin. Transfer to a heated serving dish and keep warm. Add the remaining 2 tablespoons butter to the skillet. Add the onion and sauté until deeply browned and almost crisp, stirring frequently. Sprinkle over the pumpkin and serve.

Note: The pumpkin may be cooked in boiling salted water about 5 minutes or until half tender before frying.

• *Variation*
FRIED PUMPKIN WITH GARLIC YOGURT SAUCE
Season the pumpkin slices with salt and coat with flour. Fry in butter and serve with Garlic Yogurt Sauce (page 214).

Pumpkin with Lentils Armenia

An unlikely combination? You won't think so when you try this delightful recipe.

Serves 4

½ cup dried lentils
1½ pounds pumpkin,
   peeled and cut into 1½-
   inch-long and ½-inch-
   thick slices
3 tablespoons butter
1 medium onion, finely
   chopped

2 tablespoons sugar or to
   taste
Salt to taste
2 tablespoons finely
   chopped parsley
1 cup unflavored yogurt

Wash the lentils in a sieve under running cold water. In a heavy saucepan combine the lentils with 4 cups water and bring to a boil over high heat. Reduce the heat and simmer about 30 minutes or until the lentils are tender but not mushy. Remove from the heat, drain, and set aside. Cook the pumpkin in lightly salted boiling water to cover until tender but still somewhat firm, not mushy. Drain and set aside.

Meanwhile, in a heavy skillet melt the butter over moderate heat. Add the onion and sauté until golden brown, stirring frequently. Add the pumpkin and lentils. Sprinkle with the sugar and salt and mix gently, being careful not to break or mash the vegetables. Simmer a few minutes until heated. Transfer to a warmed serving dish, sprinkle with the parsley, and serve with a bowl of the yogurt on the side.

Pumpkin with Apricots Armenia

Pumpkin and apricots enjoy a natural affinity, as the following recipe demonstrates.

Serves 4

3 tablespoons butter
1 medium onion, finely
  chopped
2 pounds pumpkin, peeled
  and cut into 1-inch
  squares
⅓ cup long-grain white
  rice, cooked in boiling

salted water until half
  tender, and drained
¾ cup dried apricots,
  chopped
¼ cup sugar or to taste
Salt to taste
¾ cup water

In an enameled saucepan melt the butter over moderate heat. Add the onion and sauté until golden brown, stirring frequently. Add the remaining ingredients and mix well. Cover and simmer about 20 minutes or until the pumpkin and rice are tender, stirring occasionally and adding more water if necessary.

• *Variation*

MASHED PUMPKIN WITH APRICOTS
Cook the pumpkin and apricots in about ½ cup water until tender. Transfer to a bowl and mash to a smooth puree. Beat in 2 tablespoons softened butter, then beat in ¼ teaspoon cinnamon (or ⅛ teaspoon each cinnamon and ginger) and sugar and salt to taste. (Some people also add a little warmed heavy cream.) Serve sprinkled with ⅓ cup finely chopped toasted walnuts or almonds.

Pumpkin with Apple

This makes a splendid accompaniment to roast turkey, ham, or pork.

Serves 4

1½ pounds pumpkin, peeled and cut into 1-inch squares
1 large tart apple, peeled, cored, and chopped
⅓ cup sugar or to taste
½ cup water
4 tablespoons butter
Salt to taste
½ cup finely chopped toasted walnuts
Cinnamon

Place the pumpkin and apple in a heavy saucepan. Sprinkle with the sugar. Add the water, butter, and salt. Cover and cook over moderate heat until the pumpkin is tender, stirring occasionally and adding more water if necessary. Transfer to a heated serving dish. Sprinkle with the walnuts and cinnamon and serve.

Spinach with Walnut Sauce

If you have never cared much for spinach, you may well change your mind when you try it this way.

Serves 4

1 pound spinach
½ cup water
Salt to taste
2 tablespoons butter
Freshly ground black pepper to taste
Walnut Sauce II (page 216)

1 medium onion, finely
 chopped

Trim the stems of the spinach. Wash carefully and chop
the leaves coarsely. Put in a saucepan with the water and
salt. Cover and simmer until the spinach is tender. Drain
thoroughly and squeeze out the moisture. Place the spinach in a mixing bowl and set aside.

Meanwhile, in a small skillet melt the butter over moderate heat. Add the onion and sauté until golden brown.
Remove from the heat and add to the spinach. Season with
the pepper. Mix lightly and let cool. Serve with the Walnut Sauce.

Fried Vegetable Platter
[Ajap Santal]

A well-thought-out and harmonious ensemble, this vegetable dish is most colorful and delectable.

Serves 4

1 medium eggplant,
 peeled and cubed
Salt
2 large green peppers,
 seeded, deribbed, and
 cut into 1- to 1½-inch
 pieces
2 medium carrots, scraped
 and sliced

Vegetable oil
Freshly ground black
 pepper, cinnamon, and
 sugar to taste
1 medium tomato, cut into
 wedges
Finely chopped fresh
 herbs to taste (parsley,
 basil, mint, and dill)

1 medium tomato, seeded and cubed	Unflavored yogurt or sour cream
1 large onion, finely chopped	White pepper to taste

Sprinkle the eggplant with salt and let stand 30 minutes. Squeeze, wash under running cold water, and dry with paper towels. Fry each vegetable separately in the oil until golden brown on all sides. Season to taste with additional salt, pepper, cinnamon, and sugar and mix gently. Mound in the center of a serving platter and garnish with the tomato wedges and herbs. Serve hot or cold, accompanied by a bowl of unflavored yogurt or sour cream seasoned with salt and white pepper to taste.

Vegetables with Egg Topping
[Borani]

This unusually imaginative combination may be enjoyed as a separate course or as a side dish.

Serves 4

1 eggplant (about 1 pound)	Butter (page 262) (approximately)
Salt	
½ pound green beans, trimmed and cut crosswise into 1½- to 2-inch lengths.	½ pound pumpkin, peeled and cut into 1½-inch-long by 1½-inch-thick slices
6 tablespoons butter, preferably Clarified	Freshly ground black pepper to taste

2 eggs
2 tablespoons finely
chopped parsley

Garlic Yogurt Sauce (page
214)

Remove the stem and hull from the eggplant. Peel and cut into cubes. Sprinkle generously with salt and let stand 30 minutes. Squeeze out the excess moisture, rinse, and dry thoroughly with paper towels. Drop the beans into boiling salted water. Boil, uncovered, about 10 minutes or until tender but still firm to the bite, not mushy. Drain and set aside.

In a heavy skillet heat 2 tablespoons of the butter over moderate heat. Add the pumpkin slices and sauté until golden brown on both sides and tender. Remove to a plate and keep warm. Add the remaining 4 tablespoons butter to the skillet and heat. Add the eggplant and sauté until lightly browned on all sides, using more butter if necessary.

Combine the vegetables in a buttered shallow baking dish about 10 inches in diameter. Sprinkle with additional salt and the pepper. Beat the eggs well with a pinch of salt and pour over the vegetables. Bake in a preheated 425° oven 5 to 10 minutes or until the eggs are firm. Sprinkle with the parsley and serve with the Garlic Yogurt Sauce on the side.

Georgian Vegetable Casserole

Serves 4

1 eggplant (about 1 pound)	fresh herbs (parsley,
3 tablespoons butter	coriander, dill, and
2 medium potatoes,	mint)
peeled and cut into	2 cloves garlic, finely
chunks	chopped
1 medium onion, finely	Freshly ground black
chopped	pepper to taste
2 tablespoons tomato paste	1 large tomato, peeled,
1 cup broth or water	seeded, and chopped
⅓ cup finely chopped	Salt to taste

Remove the stem and hull from the eggplant. Peel, cut into 1½-inch cubes, and set aside. In a heavy casserole heat 2 tablespoons of the butter over moderate heat. Add the potatoes and fry until golden brown on all sides. Remove to a plate and set aside. Add the remaining 1 tablespoon butter to the casserole, and when melted add the onion and sauté until golden brown, stirring frequently. Dissolve the tomato paste in the broth and pour into the casserole. Add the fried potatoes, eggplant, herbs, garlic, and pepper. Cover and simmer 20 minutes. Stir in the tomato and salt and cook about 10 minutes or until the vegetables are tender. Serve as a side dish with meat or poultry.

Sautéed Quinces

Serves 4

2 large quinces
2 tablespoons butter,
  preferably Clarified
  Butter (page 262)

Sugar and cinnamon to
  taste

Wash, core, and slice the quinces lengthwise, but do not peel them. In a heavy skillet heat the butter over moderate heat. Add the quince slices and sauté a few minutes. Sprinkle with the sugar and cinnamon and continue to sauté until golden brown and glazed on both sides. Serve as an accompaniment to fried or roast chicken, turkey, or pork.

Glazed Quinces

Serves 4

2 medium quinces
4 tablespoons butter,
  preferably Clarified
  Butter (page 262)

Sugar or brown sugar to
  taste
½ cup water

Wash, peel, and halve the quinces lengthwise. Carefully remove the seeds and hard core. Arrange them cut sides up in a heavy saucepan. Place ½ tablespoon of the butter on each half and sprinkle the sugar over the fruit. Add the remaining 2 tablespoons butter and the water to the saucepan. Cover and simmer about 40 minutes or until the quinces are tender and glazed, basting occasionally with the liquid in the pan. Serve as an accompaniment to fried or roast chicken, turkey, or pork.

Baked Quinces

Serves 4

4 medium quinces	⅓ cup sugar or brown
5 tablespoons melted	sugar
butter	Cinnamon to taste

Wash and peel the quinces. Cut off "lids" from the stem ends and core them to within ½ inch of the bottoms. Brush the quinces with some of the melted butter and arrange them side by side in a shallow greased baking dish just large enough to hold them comfortably in one layer. Sprinkle the cavities and surfaces of the fruit generously with a mixture of the sugar and cinnamon. Replace the "lids." Bake in a preheated 350° oven about 1 hour and 15 minutes or until tender, brushing occasionally with additional melted butter and sprinkling with more sugar and cinnamon if desired. Serve hot as an accompaniment to roasted poultry, meats, or pilafs, or serve chilled as a dessert with Pomegranate Syrup (page 219), cherry sauce, or whipped cream.

• *Variation*
BAKED APPLES
Substitute 4 tart baking apples for the quinces.

12. PICKLED VEGETABLES AND FRUITS

Homemade pickles are almost always served with a Caucasian meal, either as an appetizer or as an accompaniment to the main course. Pickles are most frequently prepared from vegetables and fruits, although they can be made from fish and meat. Some pickles are ready to eat within a matter of days; others mature slowly and keep for a considerable length of time. Pickled apricots, berries, grapes, pears, plums, eggplants, green peppers, cucumbers, and cabbage are Caucasian favorites.

The many interesting varieties and combinations of these piquant preparations certainly enhance a meal and are particularly welcome in hot weather since they stimulate the appetite and promote digestion.

Pickled Beets Georgia

Makes about 1 quart

2 pounds beets
1 cup wine vinegar
1 teaspoon salt
3 tablespoons sugar or to
    taste

5 peppercorns
4 whole cloves
½ bay leaf

Cut the tops from the beets, leaving 1 inch of the stems.
Wash the beets. Do not peel. Combine the beets with boiling water to half cover them. Cover and cook about 45
minutes or until they are tender but still somewhat firm,
not mushy. Add boiling water as needed. When done,
drain the beets, reserving 1 cup of the beet liquid. Plunge
the beets into cold water. Peel off the skins and cut the
beets into thick slices. Place them in a sterilized glass jar.
In a saucepan combine the reserved beet liquid and the
remaining ingredients and bring to a boil. Pour over the
beets, covering them completely. Seal the jar. Serve the
beets chilled.

Pickled Cabbage Georgia

Serves 4 to 6

1 medium white cabbage,
    trimmed
1 boiled beet, peeled and
    cut into 1-inch pieces
½ cup chopped celery,

2 1-inch pieces hot red
    pepper (optional)
2 bay leaves
1 teaspoon paprika
½ cup red wine vinegar

including the leaves   1½ cups boiling water
10 sprigs parsley

Remove the outer leaves from the cabbage. Quarter it. Place in a heavy saucepan and cover with cold water. Bring to a boil over high heat. Reduce the heat to low and simmer, partially covered, 10 minutes. Drain thoroughly. Cut the cabbage into chunks; do not shred it. Pack into a clean large jar with the beet, celery, parsley, pepper, bay leaves, and paprika. Mix together the vinegar and boiling water. Cover the cabbage with the solution and seal the jar. Store at room temperature 3 days, then refrigerate. To serve, remove the cabbage from the jar and drain thoroughly. Arrange on a platter and serve cold.

Pickled Cucumbers

Makes about 1 quart

2 pounds small, firm
   pickling cucumbers
2 small cloves garlic,
   sliced
8 sprigs fresh coriander
8 sprigs fresh tarragon
1 small hot red pepper,
   seeded and chopped
   (optional)

3 cups water
1 cup white wine vinegar
6 tablespoons salt (not
   iodized)
3 bay leaves
3 peppercorns
5 aromatic peppercorns
   (page 263) (optional)

Wash the cucumbers well. Pack into a clean, large glass jar with the garlic, coriander, tarragon, and red pepper interspersed at regular intervals. In a saucepan combine the remaining ingredients. Bring to a boil. Cool and pour over the cucumbers, covering them completely. Seal and store 2 weeks before using.

• *Variation*
SALTED CUCUMBERS
Pack the washed cucumbers in the jar with the garlic and sprigs of fresh dill. Bring 4 cups water and ¼ cup salt to a boil, stirring to dissolve the salt. Cool slightly, then pour over the cucumbers. Seal and store 1 week before using.

Pickled Stuffed Eggplants Armenia

Makes about 2 quarts

2 pounds very small pickling eggplants
2 medium carrots, finely chopped
2 green peppers, seeded, deribbed, and finely chopped
¼ cup finely chopped fresh coriander leaves
¼ cup finely chopped fresh mint leaves
1 clove garlic, finely chopped
2 cups water
2 cups white wine vinegar
¼ cup salt (not iodized)

Wash the eggplants. Cook them in boiling salted water 5 to 10 minutes or until slightly softened. Drain and cool under running cold water. Gently squeeze to remove all water. Mix together the carrots, green peppers, coriander, mint, and garlic. Make a small lengthwise incision on one side

of each eggplant. Stuff with a little of the vegetable mixture. Tie securely with strong white thread. Pack the eggplants compactly into clean jars. Mix together the water,
vinegar, and salt. Cover the eggplants with this solution
and seal the jars. The eggplants will be ready to eat in
about 2 weeks.

• *Variations*
One variation uses a stuffing of 1 cup minced celery,
½ cup minced green pepper, ½ cup minced parsley, and 2
cloves minced garlic. Another version uses 2 minced carrots, 1 cup minced cabbage, ½ cup minced parsley, and 2
cloves minced garlic. Several peppercorns are added to
the jar and the pickled eggplants are eaten with olive oil
added to taste.

STUFFED EGGPLANTS IN OIL (Magadinosy)
Slit the eggplants as above. Scoop out some of the pulp.
Chop it finely and combine it with 1 cup minced walnuts,
3 tablespoons minced parsley, and 2 cloves minced garlic.
Stuff the eggplants with the mixture. Fry on all sides in
sunflower seed or olive oil. Pack in a clean jar. Pour the
frying oil over the eggplants. Leave for 2 or 3 days or until
the eggplants absorb the oil. When the oil decreases, add
more oil to cover the eggplants completely. Seal the jars
and store in a cool place. The eggplants will be ready to
eat in about 10 days.

Pickled Mixed Vegetables Armenia

Makes 2 quarts

½ pound small whole
pickling cucumbers
½ pound small green
pickling tomatoes
4 small carrots, quartered
lengthwise and cut into
3- to 4-inch pieces
2 sweet green peppers,
seeded, deribbed, and
thickly sliced
2 beets, peeled and sliced
2 large cloves garlic,
sliced
8 sprigs each fresh

coriander, basil, and
tarragon
3 cups water
1 cup white wine vinegar
6 tablespoons salt (not
iodized)
3 peppercorns
3 bay leaves
1 cinnamon stick, 1 inch
long, or ¼ teaspoon
cloves (optional)
5 aromatic peppercorns
(page 263) (optional)

Wash the vegetables and pack into 2 sterilized quart jars,
adding 1 clove garlic and 4 sprigs each coriander, basil,
and tarragon to each jar. In a saucepan combine the remaining ingredients. Bring to a boil and pour over the vegetables in the jars, covering them completely. Seal and
store in a cool place 1 month.

Pickled Mixed Fruits

Makes about 3 quarts

4 pounds fresh fruit
  (apricots, plums, grapes,
  pears, peaches, and
  strawberries or
  raspberries)
2 cups water

1½ cups sugar
2 cups wine vinegar
1 teaspoon whole cloves
1 stick cinnamon or 1
  teaspoon cardamom
  seeds

Select small, firm fruit. Wash carefully. Prick the apricots and plums in several places with a toothpick. Peel and quarter the pears and peaches. Plunge the berries into boiling water. Drain and cool. Cover them with cold water 10 minutes, then drain.

Arrange the fruit in sterilized jars. In a small saucepan bring the remaining ingredients to a boil, stirring to dissolve the sugar. Boil 7 minutes. Remove from the heat and let cool slightly. Pour over the fruit, filling the jars to within ¼ inch of the top. Seal. Store in a cool place several days before using. Serve with fish, poultry, meat, and game.

Brandied Peaches Armenia
[Imbeli Oghiov yev Teghtzov]

Makes about 2 quarts

2 quarts firm peaches   1 cup water
2½ cups sugar   ¾ cup brandy

Rub away the fuzz from the peaches with a soft brush or coarse towel. Halve the peaches and remove the pits. In a large saucepan bring the sugar and water to a boil over high heat, stirring to dissolve the sugar. Reduce the heat and simmer 15 minutes or until thickened. Add the peach halves and simmer 5 to 10 minutes or until the peaches are just tender. Remove the saucepan from the heat. Place the peaches in sterilized jars. Add the brandy to the syrup in the saucepan and mix well. Pour over the fruit, filling the jars to within ¼ inch of the tops. Seal. Store in a cool, dark place.

• *Variation*
BRANDIED PEARS
Substitute peeled and cored pear halves for the peaches. Simmer them in the syrup about 30 minutes or until just tender before placing them in the jars.

13. SAUCES

In contrast to their position in Armenian and Azerbaidzhani cookery, sauces play a leading role in the Georgian cuisine. The two most famous Georgian sauces are *satsivi* (Walnut Sauce, page 215), which is used on fish, poultry, vegetables, and salads, and *tkemali* (Sour Plum Sauce, page 218), made from tart wild plums. Other Georgian sauces include *bazha*, also based on walnuts, and those made with tomatoes, garlic, barberries, grapes, pomegranates, and yogurt.

Although some of these sauces are used in the preparation of certain Armenian and Azerbaidzhani recipes, in the majority of cases the dish and its sauce are prepared together, the sauce forming an integral part of the whole rather than an independent creation that may be served separately.

Cinnamon Yogurt Sauce

Makes 1 cup

1 cup chilled unflavored
    yogurt
2 teaspoons sugar or to
    taste (optional)

1 teaspoon cinnamon

Pour the yogurt into a chilled serving bowl. Add the sugar and mix well. Sprinkle the top with the cinnamon. This sauce is served with some meat *dolmas* and is particularly good with Grapevine Leaves Stuffed with Meat and Rice (page 132).

Garlic Yogurt Sauce

Makes 1 cup

1 cup unflavored yogurt
1 clove garlic or to taste

¼ teaspoon salt

Pour the yogurt into a bowl. Pound the garlic with the salt. Add to the yogurt and stir until well blended. Cover and refrigerate several hours. Serve with fried vegetables, some lamb dishes, and some meat *dolmas*.

• *Variation*
1 teaspoon minced fresh mint leaves or ½ teaspoon crushed dried mint and 1 minced scallion, including 2 inches of the green tops, may be added to the sauce.

Walnut Sauce I Georgia
[Satsivi]

Makes about 2½ cups

2 tablespoons butter
3 tablespoons finely
   chopped onion
2 to 3 medium cloves
   garlic, finely chopped
1 tablespoon flour
1½ cups chicken broth
2 tablespoons red wine
   vinegar
⅛ teaspoon cinnamon

⅛ teaspoon ground cloves
⅛ teaspoon powdered
   saffron
2 tablespoons finely
   chopped parsley
1 bay leaf
1 cup shelled walnuts,
   ground
Salt and cayenne to taste

In a heavy saucepan melt the butter over moderate heat. Add the onion and garlic and sauté until just golden, stirring frequently. Sprinkle with the flour and stir until well blended. Add the broth and bring to a boil. Cook until the sauce is slightly thickened and smooth, stirring constantly. Add the remaining ingredients, mix well, and simmer 5 minutes. Remove the bay leaf. Serve hot with poultry and vegetables.

Note: 1 beaten egg yolk may be added to the sauce at the end. Stir well and heat. Do not boil.

Walnut Sauce II Georgia
[Satsivi]

Makes about 1½ cups

1 cup shelled walnuts
1 large clove garlic or to
taste
Salt to taste
¼ cup wine vinegar
½ cup chicken broth or
water

¼ cup finely chopped
onion (optional)
3 tablespoons finely
chopped fresh coriander
leaves or 1 teaspoon
ground coriander
Cayenne to taste

Pound the walnuts to a paste with the garlic and salt. Stir in the vinegar and broth until well blended. Add the onion, coriander, and cayenne and mix thoroughly. If necessary a little more broth may be added. Taste for seasoning. This is an excellent sauce for vegetables and salads.

Note: Fresh mint leaves or parsley may be substituted for the coriander. Fresh pomegranate juice is sometimes used instead of the wine vinegar.

Garlic Sauce

Makes 1 cup

1 clove garlic or more
½ teaspoon salt or to taste
1 cup boiling chicken or
    meat broth

½ tablespoon finely
    chopped parsley
    (optional)

Pound the garlic to a paste with the salt. Add the broth and parsley and blend well. Pour into a heated serving bowl. Serve with poultry or lamb.

Sour Plum Sauce
[Tkemali]

A Georgian classic that accompanies *shashlik* or *tabaka*.

Makes about 1½ cups

1½ cups water
½ pound sour plums
1 clove garlic
3 tablespoons finely
  chopped fresh coriander
  leaves

1 tablespoon finely
  chopped fresh basil
¼ teaspoon salt
⅛ teaspoon cayenne

In a small saucepan bring the water to a boil over moderate heat. Add the plums, cover, and cook about 20 minutes or until soft. Drain, reserving the liquid. Cut out and discard the plum pits. In the container of an electric blender combine the plums, garlic, and ¼ cup of the reserved plum liquid. Blend, gradually adding more plum liquid as needed until the mixture attains the consistency of sour cream. Return the sauce to the saucepan. Stir in the remaining ingredients. Bring to a boil over high heat. Remove from the heat and allow to cool.

Pomegranate Syrup
[Narsharab]

A brilliant ruby-red syrup with a very special sweet-sour taste, *narsharab* is traditionally served with *shashlik* but makes a marvelous accompaniment to grilled or fried fish and eggplant as well.

Makes about ¾ cup
8 pomegranates
½ cup sugar

Wash the pomegranates, cut them, and extract the juice as you would from oranges. Strain the juice and pour it into an enameled saucepan. Add the sugar and bring to a boil, stirring constantly until the sugar dissolves. Simmer, stirring occasionally, until the mixture thickens to a syrup and is reduced to about ⅓ the original amount. Skim off any froth as it rises to the surface. Remove from the heat and cool. Pour into a sterilized bottle. Store in a cool, dry place.

Note: For a novel drink, combine about 1 tablespoon pomegranate syrup or to taste with a cup of ice-cold water, soda water, lemonade, milk, or tea in the container of a blender. Cover and process until thoroughly blended. *Narsharab* can also be used as a topping for vanilla ice cream or puddings.

14. BREADS

Through the centuries bread has been accorded the highest place in the diet of Armenians, Azerbaidzhanis, and Georgians, who consider it sacred and regard it with reverence. To a Caucasian a meal without bread is unthinkable. A variety of delicious breads are eaten, with over forty different kinds made in Armenia alone.

The oldest and most classic bread of the Caucasus is thin, crisp, and cracker-like and is known as *lavash*. Its high nutritional content, great versatility, outstanding keeping qualities, and manner of preparation make it perhaps the best method yet devised of baking bread. *Lavash* has been baked the same way for many centuries in a brick-lined outdoor pit called a *tonir* or, as the Georgians call it, *toné*.

Besides the legendary *lavash* there are other classic breads such as *matnakash, peda,* and *churek,* all yeast breads, and *mchadi* (corn bread) and *deda's puri* (mother's bread), both Georgian specialties. *Mchadi* is a round, flat peasant bread made from finely ground cornmeal mixed with water and salt and sometimes stuffed with cheese. It is preferably eaten hot while soft and somewhat moist, for once cooled it hardens and is no longer as appetizing. Unlike *mchadi,* which is quickly made, *deda's puri* is baked in a *toné* like *lavash* and requires time and care in its preparation. Whole-grain, stone-ground, mountain-grown wheat is mixed with water, salt, and starter saved from a previous batch of bread, kneaded, and left to rise. When the dough is ready, it is shaped into slightly elliptical loaves. Each loaf is slapped against the inner surface of the primitive but efficient oven and adheres there until it is baked through.

Today in the cities and towns of the Caucasus, bread is not usually baked at home but is purchased from bakeries.

Caucasian Thin Bread
[Lavash]

Lavash can be made into small rounds or ovals or rolled out to a diameter of sixteen inches or more. It is most commonly made with all-purpose flour, although there is a variation using whole wheat flour. This thin, crisp bread may be broken into pieces and eaten like crackers or softened and wrapped around cheese, meat, or other foods to make a leakproof sandwich, in which case it is first sprinkled on both sides with water and wrapped in a towel for a half hour or so.

Lavash keeps long without becoming moldy. In areas of

the Caucasus where rural customs are retained, it is baked
in three- or four-months' supplies. *Lavash* is beginning to
become known in this country and is marketed commercially in large rounds up to two feet in diameter. However,
the homemade version is thinner and superior in flavor
and texture.

Makes 12

1¼ cups warm water (110°
  to 115°)
½ package active dry yeast
½ teaspoon sugar

3½ cups all-purpose flour
  (approximately)
1½ teaspoons salt

Pour ¼ cup of the water into a small bowl and sprinkle
with the yeast and sugar. Let stand 2 minutes or so, then
stir to dissolve the yeast completely.

Sift the flour and salt into a deep bowl. Make a well in
the center and pour in the yeast mixture and the remaining
1 cup water. Beginning at the center, with a large wooden
spoon gradually stir the ingredients together until well
blended. Beat in more water or flour as necessary, a little
at a time, until a firm dough is formed. Knead in the bowl
or on a lightly floured surface about 15 minutes, sprinkling
occasionally with just enough flour to keep it from sticking, until the dough is smooth and elastic. Form into a
ball. Place in a lightly oiled bowl and turn the dough to
coat with the oil. Cover loosely with a kitchen towel and
leave to rise in a warm place (85°) that is free from drafts
(such as an unlit oven with a pan of hot water on the bottom
rack) about 2 to 3 hours or until the dough doubles in size.

Punch down the dough and divide into 12 equal parts.
Form each into a ball and place 2 inches apart on a lightly
floured surface. Cover with a kitchen towel and let rest at
room temperature 30 minutes. Roll out each ball into a
very thin sheet approximately 9 to 10 inches in diameter,
occasionally sprinkling lightly with flour to keep it from

sticking. Place on an ungreased baking sheet. Prick the surface of the dough in 4 or 5 places with a fork. Bake in a preheated 375° oven about 6 to 7 minutes or until lightly browned and puffy, watching closely to prevent burning. Cool the breads on a rack. Stack them and store in a dry place.

Serve the *lavash* crisp or, about 30 minutes before serving, sprinkle it lightly with water, or hold the bread briefly under running water, then shake off the excess. Wrap in a kitchen towel and set aside to absorb the water and soften.

Note: 2 to 4 tablespoons melted butter or margarine, cooled to lukewarm, may be added with the yeast mixture and 1 cup water before blending with the flour.

White Bread with Sesame Seeds
Armenia
[Peda]

A versatile bread made in a variety of sizes and shapes, *peda* is particularly good for dipping into meat or vegetable juices. Or you may split it and stuff it with kebabs or other foods.

Makes 4

1¼ cups warm milk (110° to 115°)
1 package active dry yeast
1 teaspoon sugar
4 cups sifted all-purpose flour (approximately)

1 teaspoon salt
4 tablespoons melted butter or margarine (lukewarm)
1 egg, beaten
Sesame seeds

Pour ¼ cup of the milk into a small bowl and sprinkle with the yeast and sugar. Let the mixture rest 2 to 3 minutes, then stir to dissolve the yeast.

Combine the flour and salt in a large mixing bowl. Make a well in the center and pour in the yeast mixture, the remaining 1 cup milk, and the butter. With a large spoon stir the center ingredients together, then gradually blend into the flour. Beat until the ingredients are thoroughly blended. Turn out the dough onto a lightly floured surface and knead about 10 minutes or until smooth and elastic, sprinkling with a little flour if necessary to keep it from sticking. Form into a ball and place in a lightly oiled bowl, turning to coat it with the oil. Cover loosely with a kitchen towel and let rise in a warm place (85°) free from drafts (such as an unlit oven with a pan of hot water on the bottom rack) about 1 hour or until doubled in size.

Punch down the dough and knead again for a minute or so, then divide into 4 equal parts. Shape each into a ball, and with a rolling pin flatten it so it is about 6 inches in diameter. Arrange the loaves 3 inches apart on greased baking sheets. With a 2-inch cookie cutter, cut a circle out of the center of each round of dough, then put the circle back into the hole. Cover and let rise again in a warm place 1 hour or until doubled in size. With a pastry brush coat the surface of the loaves with the beaten egg and sprinkle generously with the sesame seeds. Bake in the center of a preheated 425° oven about 20 minutes or until golden brown. Transfer the loaves to wire racks and let cool before serving.

Note: You may substitute 3½ cups unbleached white flour and ½ cup whole wheat flour for the all-purpose flour, and 1¼ cups warm water for the milk.

Holiday Bread
[Churek or Choereg]

This great favorite may be made in various sizes, shapes, and flavors. It is usually prepared in large quantities to be served at informal gatherings or at teatime. It is also delicious with morning coffee.

Makes 4

¼ cup warm water (110° to 115°)

1 package active dry yeast

1¼ cups milk, scalded and cooled to lukewarm

2 eggs, slightly beaten

1 cup butter or margarine, melted and cooled

⅓ cup sugar

1 teaspoon salt

2 teaspoons ground aniseed

1½ teaspoons double-acting baking powder

6 cups sifted all-purpose flour (approximately)

1 egg, beaten

Sesame seeds or chopped blanched almonds

Pour the warm water into a large bowl and sprinkle it with the yeast. Let the mixture stand 2 minutes or so, then stir to dissolve the yeast. Add the milk, 2 eggs, melted butter, sugar, salt, aniseed, and baking powder and blend well. Gradually stir in the flour to make a soft dough. Turn out onto a lightly floured surface and knead about 3 minutes or until smooth. Place the dough in a lightly oiled bowl, turning it over to grease the top. Cover with a kitchen towel and let rise in a warm place (85°) free from drafts (such as an unlit oven with a pan of hot water on the bottom rack) about 2 hours or until doubled in size.

Punch down the dough and transfer it to a lightly floured surface. Divide the dough into quarters, then divide each quarter into 3 equal pieces. To shape each loaf, roll 3 pieces of dough into ropes each 12 inches long. Braid them together and pinch the ends. Arrange the loaves on lightly oiled baking sheets, cover, and let rise in a warm place about 50 minutes or until nearly doubled in size. Brush the loaves with the remaining egg and sprinkle with the sesame seeds. Bake in a preheated 350° oven about 30 minutes or until golden brown and baked through. Serve, preferably warm, with butter.

● *Variation*
For smaller *chureks* you may divide the dough into quarters, then divide each quarter into 8 equal pieces. Form each piece into simple, braided, or snail-shaped rolls. Arrange the rolls 2 inches apart on a greased baking sheet, cover, and let rise in a warm place about 50 minutes or until nearly doubled in size. Brush with the remaining egg and sprinkle with the sesame seeds. Bake in a preheated 350° oven about 20 minutes or until golden brown. Makes 32 rolls.

Note: Other common flavorings for *churek* include *mahlab* (a spice derived from black cherry kernels), vanilla, cinnamon, and grated lemon or orange rind.

Azerbaidzhani Saffron Bread

An unusual and delicately flavored bread.

Makes 4

½ cup warm milk (110° to
    115°)
1 package active dry yeast
2 eggs, slightly beaten
6 tablespoons butter,
    melted and cooled
¾ cup sifted
    confectioners' sugar

¼ teaspoon salt
⅛ teaspoon powdered
    saffron dissolved in 1
    tablespoon hot water
2½ cups sifted all-purpose
    flour (approximately)
1 egg, beaten

Pour the warm milk into a large bowl and sprinkle with
the yeast. Let the mixture stand 2 minutes or so, then stir
to dissolve the yeast. Add the 2 eggs, melted butter, confectioners' sugar, salt, and the dissolved saffron and blend
well. Gradually stir in the flour to make a soft dough. Turn
out onto a lightly floured surface and knead 10 minutes or
until smooth. Place the dough in a lightly oiled bowl, turning it over to grease the top. Cover with a kitchen towel
and let rise in a warm place (85°) free from drafts (such as
an unlit oven with a pan of hot water on the bottom rack)
about 1½ to 2 hours or until doubled in size.

Punch down the dough and transfer it to a lightly
floured surface. Divide the dough into 4 equal pieces.
Form each into a ball, and with a rolling pin flatten to
about ½-inch thickness. Arrange the loaves 3 inches apart
on lightly oiled baking sheets. Brush with the beaten egg
and decorate the tops with the tines of a fork, if desired.
Cover and let rise in a warm place 30 minutes or until
nearly doubled in size. Bake in a preheated 375° oven

about 10 to 15 minutes or until golden brown and baked through.

Note: The traditional design for this bread is a circle divided into quarters with a curl in each quarter.

Spice Bread Armenia
[Nazuk]

Here is an aromatic and uniquely delicious bread to serve for brunch or afternoon tea.

Makes 4

¼ cup warm milk (110° to 115°)
1 package active dry yeast
2 eggs, slightly beaten
6 tablespoons butter, melted and cooled
6 tablespoons sugar
½ teaspoon salt
2 to 3 teaspoons cinnamon
1 teaspoon vanilla
⅛ teaspoon powdered saffron dissolved in 1 tablespoon hot water
2½ cups sifted all-purpose flour (approximately)
1 egg, beaten

Pour the warm milk into a large bowl and sprinkle with the yeast. Let the mixture stand 2 minutes or so, then stir to dissolve the yeast. Add the 2 eggs, melted butter, sugar, salt, cinnamon, vanilla, and the dissolved saffron and blend well. Gradually stir in enough flour to make a soft dough. Turn out onto a lightly floured surface and knead about 10 minutes or until smooth. Place the dough in a lightly oiled bowl, turning it over to grease the top. Cover with a kitchen towel and let rise in a warm place (85°) free from drafts (such as an unlit oven with a pan of hot water on the bottom rack) about 1½ to 2 hours or until doubled in size.

Punch down the dough and transfer it to a lightly floured surface. Divide the dough into 4 equal pieces. Form each into a ball, and with a rolling pin flatten to about ½-inch thickness. Arrange the loaves 2 inches apart on lightly oiled baking sheets. Brush with the beaten egg. Cover and let rise in a warm place 30 minutes. Bake in a preheated 375° oven about 10 to 15 minutes or until golden brown and baked through.

Note: Other types of *nazuk* include a version made with salt and another, more complicated pastry which has a crumbly stuffing of butter, flour, saffron, and sugar or salt, depending on whether a sweet or salty *nazuk* is desired.

15. DESSERTS

Fruits, fresh or dried, singly or in combination, constitute the most typical Caucasian dessert as well as a popular between-meal refreshment. The tree-ripened fruits of the Caucasus are legendary: succulent, crisp mountain apples, pears temptingly ripe and full of nectar, peaches with an intense, almost passionate flavor, lusciously sweet figs, glowing cherries, fragrant apricots, and other exceptional fruits, including such familiar standbys as melons, grapes, plums, strawberries, raspberries, blackberries, and currants as well as the more unusual pomegranates, quinces, persimmons, mulberries, and cornelian cherries.

Fresh fruits are served artistically arranged on exquisitely hand-tooled copper trays or enormous platters, sometimes accompanied by cheese. In winter a compote of dried fruits or a bowl of dried fruits and nuts such as apricots, peaches, pears, figs, raisins, dates, walnuts, and almonds may replace the fresh fruits. Occasionally a compote of fresh fruits, a cooked fruit dessert, or a pudding based on rice or cornstarch ends a meal.

Even though Caucasians do not as a rule eat elaborate pastries and cakes at the end of their meals, they are nevertheless great connoisseurs of sweets, which are usually enjoyed with midafternoon or late-evening tea or coffee and on special occasions.

Many-Layered Pastry with Nuts and Honey Syrup
[Pakhlava]

One of the ultimate treats of the world, this sublime pastry of well-deserved fame occupies a place of honor in the Caucasian repertory.

Before making this recipe please read the entry for filo in the Glossary.

Makes 1 9-by-13-inch pastry
FILLING
3 cups finely chopped or
  ground walnuts or
  blanched almonds

¼ cup superfine sugar
1½ teaspoons ground
  cardamom or cinnamon

PASTRY
1½ cups melted Clarified
  Butter (page 262)
  (approximately)

1 pound filo pastry sheets

SYRUP

1½ cups sugar
¾ cup water
1 tablespoon freshly

squeezed and strained
lemon juice
1 tablespoon honey

Combine the filling ingredients in a bowl. Mix well and set aside. Brush a 9-by-13-by-2-inch baking pan with some of the melted butter. Cut the filo pastry sheets to fit the pan. Line the pan with half of the sheets, brushing each with butter. Spread the nut mixture evenly over the entire surface. Top with the remaining pastry sheets, brushing each with butter. With a sharp knife, cut the pastry into vertical strips 2 inches apart, then cut diagonally into diamond shapes. Bake in a preheated 350° oven 30 minutes. Reduce the heat to 300° and bake 1 hour and 30 minutes or until the pastry is light gold in color, puffed, and baked through.

Meanwhile, prepare the syrup: Combine the sugar, water, and lemon juice in a small saucepan. Bring to a boil, stirring constantly to dissolve the sugar. Cook briskly, uncovered, about 5 minutes or until the syrup reaches a temperature of 220° on a candy thermometer. Remove the pan from the heat and stir in the honey. Let it cool to lukewarm. When the *pakhlava* is done, remove it from the oven and let it cool slightly. Spoon the syrup evenly over the entire surface. Allow to cool to room temperature before serving.

Note: Any leftover pieces of pastry may be layered as evenly as possible in the pan along with the cut pastry sheets and brushed with butter. Warmed honey may be substituted for the above syrup. Some Azerbaidzhanis brush the top of the *pakhlava* with a beaten egg yolk mixed with 1 teaspoon saffron water before baking it. Each diamond may be topped with a blanched almond or unsalted pistachio nut, halved lengthwise, before baking it, or the baked *pakhlava* may be sprinkled with chopped pistachios before serving.

Armenians also make *pakhlava* with a custard or cheese filling. The cheese used should be a mild one, such as sweet Muenster or Monterey Jack.

Walnut Butter Cookies
[Kurabieh]

A traditional and classically elegant cookie which is offered on holidays and festive occasions.

Makes about 4 dozen

1 cup butter
⅓ cup confectioners' sugar
1 egg yolk, lightly beaten
½ teaspoon vanilla
½ cup walnuts, finely chopped

½ teaspoon double-acting baking powder
2¼ cups all-purpose flour, sifted
½ cup confectioners' sugar

Cream the butter until very light and fluffy. Gradually beat in the ⅓ cup confectioners' sugar. Beat in the egg yolk and vanilla. Stir in the walnuts. Sift together the baking powder and flour. Add to the butter mixture, a little at a time, until thoroughly blended. Form the dough into small sticks, sausage shapes, or balls. Place the cookies 1 inch apart on an ungreased baking sheet. Bake in a preheated 350° oven about 20 minutes or until golden and set. Remove from the oven and cool slightly. Sift the ½ cup confectioners' sugar over the cookies to cover them completely. Cool before storing.

Note: For a splendid touch sprinkle the cookies with rose water before covering them with the confectioners' sugar. One Azerbaidzhani variation known as *Baku Kurabieh* omits the walnuts. The cookies are filled with a sweetened apricot or apple puree before baking. Another version, *Zakataly Kurabieh*, uses a flavoring of honey and ground cloves rather than vanilla.

Ear-Shaped Pastries Armenia
[Akandj]

A light, delicately flavored, and decorative pastry with an unusual shape.

Serves 8

2 eggs	½ teaspoon vanilla
2 cups sifted all-purpose flour	Cognac
1 teaspoon double-acting baking powder	Vegetable oil for deep frying
Pinch salt	Confectioners' sugar

In a mixing bowl combine the eggs, flour, baking powder, and salt and mix until well blended. Add the vanilla and enough Cognac to make a dough that can be rolled. On a lightly floured board, roll out the dough into a thin sheet. Cut into half-moon shapes with a pastry cutter. With your thumb and forefinger, pinch together the center of the straight edge of each half-moon to make an "ear-shaped" pastry. Or cut the dough into circles about 2 inches in diameter and make 3 slits down the center of each circle. A third way is to cut the dough into strips about ¾ inch wide and 2 inches long and twist the ends.

Lower several pastries at a time into deep hot oil and cook until golden brown on both sides. Do not overcrowd the saucepan and take care not to burn the pastries. Lift from the oil and drain on absorbent paper. Sprinkle with the confectioners' sugar.

Yogurt Fritters in Syrup

Serves 8

SYRUP

1 cup sugar
⅔ cup water
1 teaspoon freshly
  squeezed and strained
  lemon juice

Small stick cinnamon
¼ cup honey

FRITTERS

4 eggs
1 cup unflavored yogurt
2 cups all-purpose flour
2 teaspoons sugar
1 tablespoon double-
  acting baking powder

1 tablespoon baking soda
Vegetable oil for deep
  frying

¼ cup finely chopped
   walnuts or unsalted
   pistachios

In a small saucepan bring the sugar, water, lemon juice,
and cinnamon to a boil over moderate heat. Cook, stirring
constantly, until the sugar dissolves. Stir in the honey and
cook, uncovered, 10 minutes. Remove from the heat and
allow to cool.

   Place the eggs and yogurt in a large bowl and beat until
well blended. Combine the flour, sugar, baking powder,
and baking soda. Add to the yogurt mixture and blend
well.

   In a deep fryer or heavy saucepan heat 4 inches of the
oil over moderate heat. Drop 1 tablespoon of the batter at a
time into the hot oil, being careful not to crowd the pan.
Fry the fritters until evenly browned on all sides, turning
frequently. With a perforated spoon remove them from the
oil and drain on absorbent paper.

   Mound the fritters on a serving platter and pour the
syrup evenly over them. Sprinkle with the nuts and serve.

Almond Sponge Cake Armenia
[Noushov Gargantag]

Serves 12
8 eggs, separated
3 cups confectioners'
   sugar
1 teaspoon vanilla

2½ cups sifted cake flour
   (approximately)
½ cup ground blanched
   almonds

Beat the egg yolks with the confectioners' sugar until thick and lemon-colored. Separately beat the egg whites until stiff. Fold the egg whites into the egg yolks. Add the vanilla and mix well. Fold in the flour, a little at a time, until the mixture is evenly blended and smooth. Do not mix too long. Spread 1 inch thick in a shallow baking pan lined with waxed paper. Sprinkle evenly with the almonds. Bake in a preheated 350° oven about 25 minutes or until a toothpick inserted in the middle of the cake comes out clean. Remove from the oven and cool. Remove the paper from the bottom of the cake before serving.

Yogurt Spice Cake Armenia
[Madzoonov Gargantag]

Serves 12

½ cup butter
1½ cups sugar
3 eggs, beaten
2 cups all-purpose flour
1 teaspoon double-acting
  baking powder

1 teaspoon baking soda
¼ teaspoon salt
1 teaspoon nutmeg
½ teaspoon cinnamon
1 cup unflavored yogurt
½ teaspoon vanilla

TOPPING

1 tablespoon butter
½ cup brown sugar
½ cup finely chopped
  walnuts

¾ cup shredded coconut
¼ cup cream
¼ teaspoon vanilla

In a large mixing bowl cream the butter and sugar until smooth. Beat in the eggs. Sift together the dry ingredients.

Add alternately with the yogurt to the butter mixture. Add the vanilla and blend well. Pour into a greased and floured 9-by-13-inch baking pan. Bake in a preheated 325° oven about 45 minutes or until a cake tester comes out clean. Remove from the oven and cool.

Meanwhile, prepare the topping: Mix together the butter and brown sugar. Add the remaining ingredients and blend well. Spread the mixture evenly over the cooled cake. Place briefly under the broiler until lightly browned, watching closely to prevent burning.

Khalva

Although not one of my favorites, *khalva* is an age-old sweet that remains popular, existing in numerous variations throughout the Caucasus, Middle East, and Central Asia.

Serves 4

1 cup sugar
½ cup water
½ cup butter, preferably Clarified Butter (page 262)

2 cups sifted all-purpose flour
Cinnamon

In a small saucepan bring the sugar and water to a boil over high heat, stirring constantly to dissolve the sugar. Remove from the heat and set aside.

In a heavy skillet melt the butter. Add the flour and cook over low heat about 15 minutes or until very lightly browned, stirring constantly. Gradually stir in the syrup until thoroughly blended. Turn onto a serving platter. Smooth the top, sprinkle with the cinnamon, and serve.

Note: Honey is sometimes substituted for the sugar syrup.

Quince Pudding Armenia
[Sergevilov Muhallebi]

An exquisite and delicate pudding punctuated with chopped nuts and dusted with cinnamon.

Serves 6

4 tablespoons cornstarch
2½ cups milk
¼ cup sugar
1 teaspoon vanilla
3 tablespoons quince jam

2 tablespoons toasted
blanched almonds,
finely chopped
Cinnamon

Dissolve the cornstarch in ½ cup of the milk. Place the remaining 2 cups milk and sugar in a heavy saucepan. Bring to a boil over high heat, stirring constantly until the sugar dissolves. Reduce the heat and add the cornstarch mixture, vanilla, quince jam, and 1 tablespoon of the almonds. Simmer until thickened, stirring constantly. Spoon the pudding into heatproof individual dessert bowls. Sprinkle the tops with the cinnamon and the remaining 1 tablespoon almonds. Serve chilled.

Stuffed Melon

Serves 4

1 medium cantaloupe
1 cup pitted and diced
    mixed fresh fruit
    (strawberries, cherries,
    peaches, pears, and
    grapes)
3 tablespoons sugar

1 tablespoon freshly
    squeezed and strained
    lemon juice
1 to 2 tablespoons port
    wine, apricot liqueur, or
    cherry liqueur

Cut a slice off the top of the melon and reserve. Remove the seeds and pulp. Scoop out the melon flesh. Dice it or scoop into little balls and place in a bowl. Add the fruit, sugar, lemon juice, and port and mix well. Fill the melon with this mixture. Cover with the reserved top and refrigerate several hours until chilled. Fill a serving bowl with crushed ice and place the melon in the ice. Remove the top and serve directly from the shell.

Quince Compote

Serve this fragrantly delicious and versatile creation either as a companion to roasts or as a dessert.

Serves 4 to 6

3 large quinces
1½ cups water
1 cup sugar
1 stick cinnamon, 1½ inches long

2 whole cloves
2 teaspoons freshly squeezed and strained lemon juice

Peel, quarter, and core the quinces. Cut each quarter into 3 slices. In a heavy saucepan bring the water and sugar to a boil over high heat, stirring constantly to dissolve the sugar. Add the quince slices and remaining ingredients, reduce the heat, and simmer about 1 hour or until the quinces are tender and have turned a pinkish orange in color. Serve cold as an accompaniment to roasted poultry and meats, or as a dessert with whipped cream.

Note: The grated rind of a lemon or orange may be substituted for the cinnamon stick and cloves.

Dried Fruit Compote
[Mirkatan]

An Armenian classic and a wintertime favorite that dates back many centuries.

Serves 6

4 cups water
1½ cups sugar
1 stick cinnamon, 2 inches long
2 lemon slices, ¼ inch thick

1 cup dried apricots
1 cup dried peaches
1 cup dried pears
¼ cup toasted walnuts, chopped
¼ cup brandy

In a heavy saucepan combine the water, sugar, cinnamon stick, and lemon slices. Bring to a boil over moderate heat, stirring constantly to dissolve the sugar. Add the dried fruit, reduce the heat, and simmer, uncovered, about 25 minutes or until the fruit is tender, stirring occasionally. With a slotted spoon remove the fruit to a heatproof serving bowl. Boil the syrup vigorously 5 to 10 minutes or until it is slightly thickened. Stir in the nuts and the brandy and pour over the fruit. Serve warm or chilled.

• *Variation*
DRIED FRUIT COMPOTE WITH CHESTNUTS
Substitute ½ pound shelled and peeled chestnuts (page 167) for the pears.

Note: 2 orange slices or the grated peel of 1 orange may be added with or substituted for the lemon slices.

16. CANDIES, NUTS, AND PRESERVES

In spite of the wide variety of candies and preserves available in shops, many Caucasians continue to make their own as they have done for centuries. Among the more unusual preserves prepared at home are those made with rose petals, mulberries, quinces, figs, melon, cornelian cherries, eggplant, pumpkin, and green walnuts. Preserves and jams are by no means confined to breakfast but are offered along with candies and nuts to visitors, accompanied by black coffee, tea, or a glass of brandy. Before sealing preserves, a piece of waxed paper cut to the size of the top of the jar is sometimes brushed with a little brandy and placed over the opening. This simple but elegant touch imparts a subtle fragrance to the contents.

Dried fruits and nuts are widely used in many Caucasian dishes in addition to being popular desserts and snacks. A typical favorite is dried peaches stuffed with a mixture of ground walnuts, sugar, cinnamon, and cardamom. Another is glazed or salted almonds, often served with wine or champagne.

Apple and Quince Paste Armenia
[Khintzorov yev Sergevilov Bastegh]

A popular cold-weather refreshment, this is an unusual old-time delicacy with excellent keeping qualities.

1 pound quinces,
   quartered and cored
½ pound tart cooking
   apples, quartered and
   cored

1 cup sugar
1 tablespoon freshly
   squeezed and strained
   lemon juice

In a heavy saucepan combine the quinces with a little water (about ½ cup) and boil 15 minutes. Add the apples and cook 15 minutes or until the fruits are very soft. Rub through a fine strainer. Return the puree to the saucepan and add the sugar and lemon juice. Cook over moderate heat, stirring with a wooden spoon, about 30 minutes or until the mixture thickens and comes away from the bottom and sides of the pan. Regulate the heat as necessary to prevent scorching. Remove from the heat and spread the mixture ½ inch thick on a wet shallow pan. Leave it to dry for several days. Cut into small squares or triangles and wrap in waxed paper or foil. Store in a cool, dry place. Serve with Eastern Coffee (page 253).

• *Variation*

Each square or triangle of fruit paste may be topped with a toasted blanched almond. Or you may spread a layer of ground toasted blanched almonds between 2 layers of paste before it is dried.

Glazed Prunes Azerbaidzhan

1¼ cups water
1¼ cups sugar
2 teaspoons freshly
   squeezed lemon juice
1 pound pitted dried
   prunes

As many blanched
   almonds as there are
   prunes
Sugar

In a heavy saucepan bring the water, sugar, and lemon juice to a boil over high heat, stirring constantly to dissolve the sugar. Reduce the heat and add the prunes. Simmer about 20 minutes or until the prunes are tender and glazed. Transfer the prunes to a plate and set aside to cool. Stuff each prune with an almond and roll in the sugar. Allow to dry several hours before storing.

• *Variation*
Substitute dried figs for the prunes.

Walnut and Date Confection

Rich, moist, and almost cakelike, this makes a fine dessert served with coffee.

Serves 4

1 cup pitted dates, ground   1 teaspoon cinnamon
1 cup ground walnuts   Whipped cream

Combine the dates, walnuts, and cinnamon and pound until thoroughly blended and smooth. Spread about ½ inch thick on a plate. Cut into diamond shapes. Serve cold, garnished with the whipped cream.

Note: Brandy or orange flower water may be substituted for the cinnamon.

Candied Almonds or Walnuts
[Kozinak or Gozinakh]

A favorite holiday confection that is served with a glass of brandy to visitors.

Serves 6

1 cup honey   ¼ teaspoon vanilla
¼ cup sugar
2 cups chopped blanched
    almonds or walnuts

Place the honey and sugar in a heavy saucepan. Bring to a boil, stirring constantly to dissolve the sugar. Cook without stirring until the syrup reaches 220° on a candy thermometer. Reduce the heat and add the nuts. Cook about 15 minutes or until the nuts turn golden brown, stirring frequently. Add the vanilla and mix well. Remove from the heat and pour onto an oiled marble slab. Smooth the top and allow to cool. When firm cut into squares.

• *Variation*
SESAME-ALMOND CANDY
Follow the above directions, using 1 cup honey, 1 cup sugar, 1 cup minced nuts, and 1 cup sesame seeds.

Roasted Walnuts

Walnuts are plentiful in the Caucasus and are a staple in the diet of Armenians, Azerbaidzhanis, and, particularly, the Georgians. Green walnuts are much appreciated for their high nutritional content and flavor. Considered a delicacy, they are enjoyed both raw and made into jam.

Place unshelled walnuts in a shallow baking pan. Roast in a preheated 425° oven about 15 minutes or until toasted through. Test by cracking one open and tasting it. Serve while still warm.

Roasted Chestnuts

Caucasians like to spend cold winter evenings around a fireplace, roasting chestnuts and telling old tales.

To ensure freshness and maximum flavor, choose heavy nuts with tight-fitting shells. With a sharp-pointed knife, make two cross-cut gashes on the flat side of each chestnut, without cutting through the meat. Place them cut sides up in a single layer on a shallow baking pan. Roast in a preheated 425° oven about 15 minutes or until the shells and inner skins can be removed. Or for an even better flavor, place the gashed nuts in a special chestnut pan or wire basket and roast over an open fire, tossing them frequently until done. Serve warm with a sweet wine.

Pumpkin Marmalade

Makes about 1 pint

4 cups sugar
2 cups water
1 tablespoon freshly
   squeezed and strained
   lemon juice

4 cups shredded pumpkin
1 teaspoon vanilla
¼ cup slivered blanched
   almonds (optional)

In a heavy enameled or stainless steel saucepan combine the sugar, water, and lemon juice. Bring to a boil over high heat, stirring constantly to dissolve the sugar. Reduce the heat and simmer until the syrup is thick enough to coat the back of a spoon. Stir in the pumpkin and simmer until it is soft and transparent, stirring occasionally and skimming off any foam as it rises to the surface. Add the vanilla and the almonds, mix well, and cook a few minutes more. Ladle into sterilized glass jars, filling them to the top. Seal at once.

• *Variation*
Instead of the vanilla, the marmalade may be flavored with cinnamon and cloves. Wrap 1 stick cinnamon in cheesecloth with 2 whole cloves. Stir into the syrup with the pumpkin. The grated rind of ½ lemon may also be added.

Quince Preserves

An exquisite preserve, delicately flavored with fragrant spices and with a touch of lemon juice to prevent it from being cloyingly sweet.

Makes about 2 pints

6 large quinces
3 cups sugar
3 cups water
1½ tablespoons freshly
   squeezed and strained
   lemon juice

1 stick cinnamon
3 whole cloves
½ cup slivered blanched
   almonds (optional)

Peel and quarter the quinces, then core and dice them. In a heavy enameled or stainless steel pot bring the sugar and water to a boil over high heat, stirring constantly to dissolve the sugar. Add the diced quinces, lemon juice, cinnamon, and cloves and bring to a boil. Reduce the heat and simmer, stirring occasionally, about 2½ hours or until the syrup is thickened. Lift out the cinnamon and cloves and stir in the almonds. Remove from the heat. Pour into sterilized jars and seal.

Fig Preserves

If you are fortunate enough to be able to obtain fresh figs, you might try this unusual and tempting Armenian delicacy.

2 pounds fresh green or
   black figs
Brandy
3½ cups sugar

2 cups water
1 tablespoon freshly
   squeezed and strained
   lemon juice

Choose small, unblemished figs. Wash and dry them carefully. Prick all over with a fork. Holding each fig by the stem, dip it in the brandy and place on a platter.

In a heavy enameled or stainless steel saucepan bring the sugar, water, and lemon juice to a boil over high heat, stirring constantly to dissolve the sugar. Reduce the heat and cook until the syrup is slightly thickened. Add the figs, remove from the heat, and let soak overnight. The next day bring to a boil and simmer until the figs are tender. Using a perforated spoon, lift out the figs and place them in sterilized jars. Continue to simmer the syrup a few minutes until it has thickened enough to coat the back of a spoon. Pour over the figs and seal.

17. BEVERAGES

Caucasians have been masters in the art of wine-making from time immemorial. The excellent grapes grown in the Caucasus form the basis of superior wines and brandies that are justly famous throughout the Soviet Union and which easily rank among the finest in the world. Unfortunately, because of limited production and distribution, bottled Caucasian wines are not well known outside the USSR.

The Caucasus produces many different kinds of red, white, and rosé table wines, fortified wines, champagne, brandy, and vodka. Wine is always served with meals, and even a casual visitor will invariably be offered a glass of wine or brandy.

The autumn grape harvest is a time of feasting and celebration. In Kakhetia, the famous wine-producing region of Georgia, the balconies and walls of the houses are covered with garlands of grapes and *chuchkella,* a traditional candy made from thickened grape juice and walnuts. The fragrance of *shashlik* fills the air, and everywhere people join together in songs and toasts, clinking their glasses of sweet foaming wine. Each community has its favorite vine and its own blend of wine.

With appetizers Caucasians serve a strong, very dry spirit distilled from grapes known as *raki*. The local beer is popular and also makes an appropriate accompaniment to Caucasian food. A favorite summer drink is *kryushon*, a kind of punch made with wine and fruits. Softer beverages include cream soda, lemonade, and *tahn*, which is yogurt diluted with cold water and salt. Refreshing beverages made with various fruit juices and syrups are also extensively consumed.

The Caucasus is noted for its mineral waters. Millions of bottles are shipped annually to all parts of the Soviet Union and exported to many foreign countries as well.

Among the hot beverages tea is a great favorite, as might be expected in a tea-producing area like the Caucasus. Often served in glasses rather than in cups, it is accompanied by cubed sugar and, frequently, lemon slices. In addition, Azerbaidzhanis are fond of cinnamon tea and ginger tea. The former is light orange in color and is made by boiling crushed cinnamon with water, straining it, and serving it with cubed sugar. The latter is a yellow tea prepared in the same manner, with ginger substituted for the cinnamon.

Coffee is also popular. Black, thick, and syrupy, it is traditionally served in small demitasse cups from which it is sipped rather than drunk.

Eastern Coffee

This coffee, known in America as Greek or Turkish coffee, is made and served from a narrow-necked, long-handled brass or enamel pot that comes in several sizes, the largest holding about five or six servings only.

Makes 1 demitasse cup

1 heaping teaspoon pulverized Turkish coffee, or more for a stronger brew

1 teaspoon sugar or to taste
1 demitasse cup fresh cold water

Combine the coffee, sugar, and water in the special coffeepot described above and stir well. Bring to a boil until the froth rises to the top of the pot. Remove from the heat immediately to avoid boiling over. Stir and return to the heat until the froth rises again. Repeat this procedure once more. Remove from the heat. Pour off the froth into a demitasse cup, then gently pour the hot coffee into the cup, taking care not to disturb the froth, which will rise to the surface. Serve at once, accompanied by a glass of ice water. Do not drink the grounds that settle at the bottom of the cup.

Note: The coffee may be flavored with a cardamom seed, which is added to the pot while the coffee is brewing.

Upon removing the pot from the heat for the last time, you may add a few drops of cold water to settle the grounds.

Iced Yogurt Drink
[Djrikhnats, Batsan Matsun, or Tahn]

A typical Armenian beverage, this is a cooling and comforting drink for a hot summer day.

Serves 4

2 cups unflavored yogurt
1½ to 3 cups ice-cold
   water

Salt to taste
Fresh mint leaves
   (optional)

Place the yogurt in a deep bowl and beat until smooth. Gradually beat in the water until thoroughly blended. Season with the salt. Alternately, the yogurt, water, and salt may be blended in an electric blender. Serve chilled over ice cubes, garnished if you like with the mint leaves.

Chilled Pomegranate Nectar

An unusual, pleasantly tart, and delightfully refreshing drink.

Serves 4

8 large pomegranates
Freshly squeezed and
   strained juice of 1 lemon

⅔ cup sugar or to taste

Wash the pomegranates and cut them into halves. Extract the juice as you would from oranges. Strain the pomegranate juice. Add the lemon juice and sugar and stir to dissolve the sugar. Chill. Serve over crushed ice.

Strawberry Syrup

Makes about 2 cups

1½ pounds strawberries, washed, drained, and hulled
4¾ cups sugar
1 tablespoon freshly squeezed and strained lemon juice
A few drops red food coloring

Place the strawberries and 2½ cups of the sugar in alternate layers in an enameled saucepan. Crush the berries to release the juice and let stand overnight. The following day stir to dissolve the sugar, then pass through a food mill or sieve, or puree in a blender. Return to the saucepan, add the remaining sugar, and bring to a boil, stirring constantly to dissolve the sugar. Reduce the heat and cook 5 minutes. Stir in the lemon juice and food coloring and remove from the heat. Strain the syrup, pour into sterilized bottles, and seal. Store in a cool place.

To serve, use 2 tablespoons syrup for each 8-ounce glass of cold water. Or mix with other fresh fruit juices. Add ice cubes. This syrup may also be served over vanilla ice cream.

Caucasian Fruit Punch
[Kryushon]

Makes about 1 quart

1 pound mixed fruit (such
   as peaches, cherries,
   strawberries, apricots, or
   other fruit)

1 bottle sweet white wine
1 ounce Cognac
Peel of ½ lemon

Stone the fruit and slice. Combine with the remaining ingredients and chill thoroughly. Serve very cold.

Sour Cherry Brandy

Makes 1 quart

4 pounds ripe sour
   cherries

4 cups sugar
1½ pints brandy or vodka

Wash the cherries in a colander under running cold water. Discard any stems or blemished fruit. Dry thoroughly with paper towels and place in a wide glass container or jar. Add the sugar. Cover the top with a piece of cheesecloth and tie it on. Let stand 30 to 40 days in a sunny spot. Strain through a fine sieve. Filter through a thin layer of cotton or a very fine cloth. Stir in the brandy. Pour into clean bottles and seal.

18. DAIRY PRODUCTS

Dairy products have always played a prominent role in Caucasian cookery. The abundance of domestic utensils unearthed by excavations, such as vessels used for the storage of butter and cheese and large pitchers for that of milk and yogurt, as well as the discovery of churns remarkably similar to those used in the Caucasus at the present time, attest to the importance of dairy products in the diet and economic life of the ancient inhabitants of the area.

Today a wide range of dairy products, both commercial and homemade, is to be found in the Caucasus, including different kinds of milk, cream, butter, yogurt, and cheese.

Armenians are especially fond of cheese, which has been a basic everyday food and a national favorite for thousands of years. Every meal, regardless of how simple or elaborate, begins and ends with it, and there is hardly a more popular snack than cheese accompanied by wine or beer. In addition, cheese is used liberally throughout the

Armenian cuisine. It is therefore not surprising that Armenians have developed many excellent cheeses that have gained a well-deserved reputation all over the USSR. Below are listed some of the most widely appreciated ones.

ARMENIAN "SWISS." This cheese, with a merited reputation throughout the Soviet Union, has a sweetish nutty taste, fine aroma, and a tender and elastic consistency.

ARMENIAN "DUTCH." Made from cow's milk, this hard, small cheese enjoys a wide distribution.

ARAKADZ. A semihard cheese with a mild nutty taste, made from sheep's milk.

ARMENIAN "ROQUEFORT." Made from both sheep's and cow's milk. The first is made exclusively in Armenia and has a buttery and molded consistency with blue-green stripes. It is sharper in taste and slightly harder than the second type.

KANATCH or *MKLATS PANIR* (**GREEN** or **MOLDED CHEESE**). The Armenian national cheese, similar to Roquefort, with a pleasant, sharp taste. It is matured in clay pots or in hides.

VAYATZOR. This cheese, which is stored in jars, is made from a mixture of sheep's and goat's milk with an addition of leavening. Herbs, seeds, and roots are added either to the leavening or directly to the cheese, giving it a distinctive flavor and aroma.

YEGHEGNATZOR. A recent cheese, first produced in 1966, similar to *vayatzor.* It has a pungent taste, contains cumin or some other spice, and has a soft and rather loose consistency.

MOTAL. Matured in hides, this sharp cheese with a pleasant aroma is made from sheep's milk or a mixture of sheep's and goat's milk. It is eaten with *lavash* and spicy fresh herbs.

BRINDZA. A very popular white, saltwater cheese similar to Greek *feta*, with a soft texture and milky taste.

CHANAKH or KLUKH PANIR (HEAD CHEESE). A very common soft cheese with a salty taste. It is made from cow's or sheep's milk, the latter being both saltier and harder.

CHILCHIL. A lean, sour, saltwater cheese that is stretched and tied into a bundle of threads. The consistency is dense and hard. Like all saltwater cheeses, it must be rinsed under running warm or cold water before being eaten.

TEL or HUSATS PANIR (STRING or BRAIDED CHEESE). Similar to *chilchil*, this is made in rural districts, generally as a table ornament and to demonstrate a housewife's culinary expertise. The strings are made as thin as possible, an art requiring much skill and experience.

Yogurt
[Matsun or Matsoni]

Yogurt is a basic food in the Caucasus, where it is made from the milk of cows, sheep, and water buffalo. That made from water buffalo milk is richer and sweeter. Yogurt is eaten plain, diluted with water to make a refreshing beverage, used as a base for soups, sauces, and salads, and even made into butter and cheese.

Makes 1 quart
1 quart milk

2 tablespoons live yogurt   commercial unflavored
  (either homemade or   yogurt)

In an enameled or flameproof glass saucepan bring the
milk to a boil, being careful not to allow it to boil over.
Remove from the heat and cool to a temperature of about
110°. Working quickly, place the live yogurt in a small
glass bowl. Gradually beat in several tablespoons of the
warm milk until well blended. Then stir this into the remaining milk in the bowl until thoroughly mixed. Pour
into a wide-mouthed thermos bottle and seal at once.
Leave undisturbed about 8 hours or overnight or until the
yogurt attains a rich, custard-like consistency. Alternately,
you may pour the mixture into a clean glass bowl. Cover
with clear plastic wrap, then cover with a kitchen towel.
Leave undisturbed in a warm place free from drafts about
8 hours. If you leave the bowl in the warmth much longer
than this, the yogurt will have an unpleasant sour taste.
Well-made yogurt is creamy and mild in flavor.

When ready, empty the yogurt into a glass jar and refrigerate. To ensure a constant supply of yogurt, always re-
member to save a few tablespoons from each batch to be
used as the starter for your next one. For best results make
a fresh batch of yogurt every 3 or 4 days.

Note: ½ to 1 cup heavy cream added to the milk before
boiling makes a richer, thicker yogurt.

Yogurt Cheese

Serves 6
1 quart Yogurt (page 259)

½ teaspoon salt
⅓ cup olive oil
2 tablespoons chopped
  fresh mint or dill

2 tablespoons finely
  chopped scallions or
  chives (optional)

Mix the yogurt and the salt and pour into a bag made of several layers of cheesecloth. Tie the bag and suspend it overnight over a bowl to catch the drippings.

When the yogurt has become firm enough to spread, remove it from the bag and shape into little balls, or turn into a serving bowl and make a depression down the center. Pour the olive oil over the balls or into the depression and sprinkle with the mint and scallions. Serve cold as an appetizer, accompanied by Caucasian Thin Bread (page 221).

Flavored Butters

Caucasians, along with most Middle Easterners, prefer to serve bread with various dips such as Eggplant Puree (page 17) rather than butter. However, I have found that any of the following flavored butters makes an admirable spread for freshly baked White Bread with Sesame Seeds (page 223) or French bread. Use fresh, good butter and serve the flavored butter in a small crock or attractive dish.

SPICED BUTTER
Combine ¼ pound soft butter with ½ teaspoon cinnamon or allspice, or ½ teaspoon cinnamon and a pinch of nutmeg, and salt to taste. Mix well.

NUT BUTTER

Follow the directions given for Spiced Butter (above), adding ½ cup very finely chopped toasted almonds or pistachios with the spices.

SESAME BUTTER

Follow the directions given for Spiced Butter (above), adding ½ cup toasted sesame seeds with the spices.

CINNAMON AND OREGANO BUTTER

Combine ¼ pound soft butter with ½ teaspoon cinnamon and 2½ teaspoons oregano. Mix well. This is also excellent spread on slices of crusty bread, which are then toasted in the oven.

Clarified Butter

Makes about ¾ pound

Clarified butter is used extensively in Caucasian cooking. Since it burns less easily than ordinary butter, it is preferred for frying and pastry-making. It is easily made and keeps well.

Place 1 pound butter, cut into pieces, in a heavy saucepan. Melt over low heat, being careful not to let it brown. Remove from the heat and skim off the foam that has risen to the surface. Let rest several minutes, then carefully strain the clear yellow liquid through a very fine sieve or through cheesecloth into a jar, leaving the milky residue in the bottom of the pan. Cover the jar tightly and refrigerate.

GLOSSARY OF SPECIAL INGREDIENTS

Abgora. The juice of sour or unripe grapes.

Albukhara. A type of plum found in the Caucasus, light yellow in color, with a firm flesh and sweet-sour taste. Excellent in sauces, relishes, jams, compotes, and for drying.

Aromatic Peppercorns. These peppercorns, sometimes called "English pepper," are dark brown in color and have a spicy aroma that suggests a blend of carnation and cinnamon. Used in soups, stews, and in pickling.

Barbaris (**Barberis, Barberry**). A very common shrub that grows in both a wild and cultivated state. When ripe, the *barbaris* berries are bright red and contain a great deal of malic and citric acid. Fresh berries are used to make jams, jellies, and syrups. Dried and powdered berries are used as a seasoning or condiment for a number of Caucasian specialties such as *shashlik* and *lyulya kebab*. Marinated berries make a pleasantly piquant accompaniment to roast meats, game, and fowl.

Basturma. (1) Dried beef seasoned with fenugreek, hot peppers, cumin, garlic, and other spices. Very popular in Armenia both as a cold cut served as an appetizer or cooked with eggs. Available in specialty shops. (2) Caucasian grilled marinated meat.

Bulghur. Cooked, dried, and cracked wheat. It comes in three sizes: fine (#1), medium (#2), and coarse (#3). Bulghur is available in bulk at Middle Eastern groceries.

Chick-Peas. Also known as *ceci* beans in Italian and *garbanzo* beans in Spanish. Canned chick-peas are sold in supermarkets. Dried chick-peas may be purchased from Middle Eastern and Mediterranean specialty shops and from some supermarkets.

Coriander. An herb resembling flat-leaf parsley but having a distinctive aroma and flavor. Fresh coriander is widely used in the Caucasus and is easily available there. In America it is also known as *cilantro* and Chinese parsley and may be purchased from Latin-American and Chinese markets.

Filo (Phyllo). Paper-thin sheets of dough used in making the many-layered Caucasian pastries such as *pakhlava*. Also known as strudel dough, this ready-made dough may be obtained from Middle Eastern groceries and bakeries and certain specialty shops. It comes by the pound in long narrow packages, each one containing about 25 or more sheets, depending on the manufacturer. Since not only the degree of thinness but the size of the sheets as well vary from brand to brand, the amount of butter and filling called for in the recipes should be adjusted accordingly. When handling filo, it is important to work quickly but carefully to prevent the delicate sheets from drying out and breaking. Any portion of dough that is not being used at a given moment must be covered with a lightly dampened kitchen towel.

Gora. Sour or unripe grapes.

Grapevine Leaves. Use freshly picked leaves or the preserved leaves sold in jars or cans at Middle Eastern groceries and specialty shops.

***Kizil* (Cornelian Cherry).** A shrub or small tree that grows wild in many areas of the Caucasus and is occasionally cultivated in gardens as well. The fruit of the *kizil* is bright red, oval in shape, tart in flavor, and has a large kernel. Used extensively in the preparation of jams, compotes, juices, syrups, fruit paste, soups, and fish and poultry dishes.

Kyurdyuk. Lamb fat taken from under the tail of a certain species of sheep bred in the Caucasus and Central Asia. *Kyurdyuk* is a basic ingredient in Caucasian, particularly Azerbaidzhani, cuisine, where it is minced or ground and added to soups and stuffings, cubed and alternated with lean meat on *shashlik* skewers, and melted and used like butter for cooking. In areas where *kyurdyuk* is unavailable, clarified or ordinary butter is substituted; however, the taste, understandably, is not the same.

Lavashana. A paste prepared from damson, *barbaris, kizil,* or other fruit. The fruit is cooked, pitted, and rubbed through a sieve. It is then spread in a thin layer to dry in the sun. *Lavashana,* or *pasteghlavash* as it is sometimes called, is used in a number of Caucasian dishes and in winter replaces fresh plums in recipes calling for the latter.

Narsharab. A tart syrup of cooked pomegranate juice. Although bottled pomegranate syrup is available in Middle Eastern groceries, homemade *narsharab* (page 219) is preferable.

Pine Nuts. The edible kernels of certain pine cones, also known as *pignoli, pignolia,* or *pignola.* They are about ½ inch long, cream-colored, and have a slightly oily taste. Pine nuts are sold in Mediterranean and Middle Eastern groceries, nut shops, health food stores, and some supermarkets.

Pomegranate. This exotic fruit has a tough reddish rind and contains numerous seeds enclosed in a juicy red pulp. In the Caucasus three types grow: sweet, sour, and sweet-sour. Pomegranates ripen in October and can be kept in a cool place about five months. They are much appreciated by Caucasians, who eat them raw and use them in cooking. The seeds may be dried for future use. In addition to making a very refreshing drink, pomegranate juice is used in preparing the popular syrup *narsharab*. The best type for *narsharab* is the sweet-sour variety.

Quince. A fragrant fruit with a tart, astringent taste and high pectin content. Various types differing in size, flavor, and consistency are grown in the Caucasus. Quinces, familiar to Americans mainly in the form of jams and jellies, are highly regarded by Caucasians, who in addition to using them for marmalades and preserves feature them in soups, poultry and meat dishes, compotes, desserts, and confections.

Raki (Chachis Araki, Oghi). A potent colorless spirit distilled from grapes and flavored with aniseed.

Rose Water. A fragrant liquid flavoring distilled from fresh rose petals. It is available at Middle Eastern groceries and some gourmet shops.

Saffron. The dried stigma of the cultivated crocus, and the world's most expensive spice. Used extensively in Caucasian, particularly Azerbaidzhani, cookery to flavor and color foods.

***Sumakh* (Sumac).** A shrub or small tree that grows wild in sparsely wooded areas of Transcaucasia. Its red, tart, and lentil-shaped berries grow in bundles. They are dried, powdered, and used as a seasoning or condiment for *shashlik* and other dishes.

SHOPPERS' GUIDE

Below is a partial list of sources for the special ingredients called for in recipes throughout this book. Some will accept mail orders. For additional sources consult your telephone directory for Armenian, Greek, and Middle Eastern groceries and bakeries, as well as gourmet food shops.

ALABAMA
Birmingham
Bruno's Food Store, 2620 13th Avenue West. 35204
Sawaya Delicatessen, 1104 South 10th Street. 35205
Mobile
Lignos Grocery, 160 Government Street. 36602

ARIZONA
Phoenix
Filippo's Italian Groceries and Liquor Wheel, 3435 East
McDowell Road. 85008

CALIFORNIA
Anaheim
Athens West, 111 North Dale Avenue. 92801
Fresno
Hanoian's Market, 1439 South Cedar Avenue. 93702
Valley Bakery, 502 M Street. 93721
Long Beach
Batista Imports, 222 East 5th Street. 90812
Los Angeles
Bezjian's Grocery, 4725 Santa Monica Boulevard. 90029
Europa Grocery Co., 321 South Spring Street. 90013
Greek Importing Co., 2801 West Pico Boulevard. 90006
Oakland
G. B. Ratto & Co. International Grocers, 821 Washington
Street. 94607
San Diego
Athens Market, 414 E Street. 92101
San Diego Importing Co., 2061 India Street. 92101
San Francisco
Haig's Delicacies, 441 Clement Street. 94118
Istanbul Pastries & Imported Foods, Ghirardelli Square,
900 North Point. 94109
Mediterranean and Middle East Import Co., 223 Valencia
Street. 94103

COLORADO
Denver
Kebab Bakery & Delicatessen, 2703 East 3rd Avenue.
80206

CONNECTICUT
Danbury
Dimyan's Market, 116 Elm Street. 06810
New Britain
Vittoria Importing Co., 35 Lafayette Street. 06051
Waterbury
Impero Import Co., Inc., 121 South Main Street. 06702

DISTRICT OF COLUMBIA
Washington
Aloupis Co., 916 9th Street N.W. 20012
Skenderis Greek Imports, 1612 20th Street N.W. 20009

FLORIDA
Miami
Arabic Grocers and Bakery, 123 S.W. 27th Avenue. 33135
Greek American Grocery Co., 2690 Coral Way. 33145
Tarpon Springs
Angel's Market, 455 Athens Street. 33589

GEORGIA
Atlanta
Foxies Delicatessen, 659 Peachtree Street N.E. 30383
George's Delicatessen, 1041 North Highland Avenue N.E.
    30312

HAWAII
Honolulu
Gourmet Bazaar, International Market Place. 96815

ILLINOIS
Chicago
Athens Grocery, 811 West Jackson Street. 60607
Columbus Food Market, 5534 West Harrison Street. 60644
Hellas Grocery Store and Pastry, 2621 and 2627 West
    Lawrence Avenue. 60625

INDIANA
Indianapolis
Athens Imported Food Store, 103 North Alabama Street.
   46204

IOWA
Des Moines
Italian Importing Co., 316 3rd Street. 50309

KENTUCKY
Louisville
A. Thomas Meat Market, 309 East Jefferson Street. 40202

LOUISIANA
New Orleans
Central Grocery Co., 923 Decatur Street. 70116
Progress Grocery Co., 915 Decatur Street. 70016

MAINE
Portland
Model Food Importers, 115 Middle Street. 04111

MARYLAND
Baltimore
H. & H. Importing Co., 518 South Broadway. 21231
Imported Foods, Inc., 409 West Lexington Street. 21201

MASSACHUSETTS
Belmont
Eastern Lamejun, 145 Belmont Street. 02178
Boston
Syrian Grocery Importing Co., 270 Shawmut Avenue.
   02118
Cambridge
Cardullo's Gourmet Shop, 6 Brattle Street. 02138

Dedham
Homsy Middle East Importing Co., 918 Providence Highway. 02026
Watertown
Aintab Lahmejune, 564 Mt. Auburn Street. 02172

MICHIGAN
Detroit
Acropolis Market, 8441 Joy Road. 48204
Delmar & Co., 501 Monroe Avenue. 48226
Southfield
American Oriental Grocery, 20736 Lahser Road. 48075

MINNESOTA
Minneapolis
The Pavo Co., Inc., 119 North 4th Street. 55401

MISSOURI
St. Louis
Heidi's Around the World Food Shop, 1149 South Brentwood Boulevard. 63117

NEBRASKA
Omaha
A. Marino Grocery, 1716 South 13th Street. 68108

NEW HAMPSHIRE
Manchester
Joseph's Brothers Market, 196 Lake Avenue. 03103
Nashua
Liamos Market, 176 West Pearl Street. 03060

NEW JERSEY
Moonachie
Sahadi Importing Co., Inc., 200 Carol Place. 07074
  (This major firm distributes its product nationwide.)

Union City
Michael Nafash & Sons, 2717 Bergenline Avenue. 07087

NEW YORK
Brooklyn
George Malko, 185 Atlantic Avenue. 11201
Buffalo
Sammy's Imported and Domestic Foods, 1348–54 Hertel
Avenue. 14126
New York City
House of Yemen East, 370 Third Avenue. 10016
K. Kalustyan Orient Export Trading Corp., 123 Lexington
Avenue. 10016
Kassos Brothers, 570 Ninth Avenue. 10036
Middle East & Oriental Grocery Store (Karnig Tashjian),
380 Third Avenue. 10016
Rochester
International Importers of Fine Foods, 845 Bull's Head
Shopping Plaza and 388 Jefferson Road. 14611 and
14623
Syracuse
Thanos Imported Grocery, 424 Pearl Street. 13203

NORTH CAROLINA
Charlotte
East Trade Company, 402 East Trade Street. 28202
Raleigh
Galanides-Raleigh, Inc., Wicker Drive and Campbell
Street. 27604

OHIO
Akron
Ellis Bakery, 577 Grant Street. 44311
Canton
Canton Importing Co., 1136 Wertz Avenue N.W. 44708
Cincinnati
Bruno Foods, 4970 Glenway Avenue. 45238

Cleveland
Sheikh Grocery Co., 652 Bolivar Road. 44115
Toledo
Antonio Sofo & Son Importing Co., 3253 Monroe Street. 43606

OKLAHOMA
Oklahoma City
Nick's Importing Co., 2416 North Western Avenue. 73106
Royal Coffee and Tea Co., 7519 North May Avenue. 73116
Tulsa
Antone's Imported Foods, 2606-K South Sheridan Road. 74129

OREGON
Portland
Downtown Delicatessen, 345 S.W. Yamhill Street. 97204
Pieri's Delicacies Inc., 3824 S.E. Powell Boulevard. 97202

PENNSYLVANIA
Philadelphia
Armenian Pizza, 6204 Woodbine Avenue. 19151
Pittsburgh
European Grocery Store, 520 Court Place. 15219
Stamoolis Brothers Co., 2020 Pennsylvania Avenue. 15233
Wilkes-Barre
Adelphia Delicatessen, 19 East Market Street. 18701

RHODE ISLAND
Providence
Near East Market, 41 Cranston Street. 02903

TENNESSEE
Memphis
Barzizza Brothers Inc., 351 South Front Street. 38103

TEXAS
Dallas
Capello's Imported & American Foods, 5328 Lemmon Avenue. 75209
Houston
Antone's Imported Co., P.O. Box 3352, 807 Taft Street, 8111 Main Street, and 1639 South Adams Street. 77001, 77019, 77025, and 77011
San Antonio
Paletta's Import Foods, 202 Recoletta Road. 78216

VIRGINIA
Norfolk
Galanides, Inc., 902 Cooke Avenue. 23504
Richmond
Greek American Importing Co., 518 East Marshall Street. 23219

WASHINGTON
Seattle
DeLaurenti Italian & International Market, 1435 First Avenue. 98101
Spokane
Gino's World Food Mart, North 126 Washington Street. 99201

WISCONSIN
Milwaukee
Topping & Co., 736 North 2nd Street. 53203

CANADA
Montreal, Quebec
Ali Baba Oriental, 2003 Laurentian Avenue
Hellenic Grocery, 5828 Park Avenue
Toronto, Ontario
Denos Giagilitsis, 221 O'Connor Drive

INDEX